MILITARY AND VETERAN ISSUES

POST-TRAUMATIC STRESS AND MENTAL HEALTH IN THE U.S. MILITARY

ISSUES AND RESPONSE EFFORTS

MILITARY AND VETERAN ISSUES

Additional books in this series can be found on Nova's website under the Series tab.

Additional E-books in this series can be found on Nova's website under the E-book tab.

PSYCHOLOGY RESEARCH PROGRESS

Additional books in this series can be found on Nova's website under the Series tab.

Additional E-books in this series can be found on Nova's website under the E-book tab.

MILITARY AND VETERAN ISSUES

POST-TRAUMATIC STRESS AND MENTAL HEALTH IN THE U.S. MILITARY

ISSUES AND RESPONSE EFFORTS

JEFFREY N. LENTZ
EDITOR

nova publishers
New York

For permission to use material from this book please contact us:
Telephone 631-231-7269; Fax 631-231-8175
Web Site: http://www.novapublishers.com

NOTICE TO THE READER

The Publisher has taken reasonable care in the preparation of this book, but makes no expressed or implied warranty of any kind and assumes no responsibility for any errors or omissions. No liability is assumed for incidental or consequential damages in connection with or arising out of information contained in this book. The Publisher shall not be liable for any special, consequential, or exemplary damages resulting, in whole or in part, from the readers' use of, or reliance upon, this material. Any parts of this book based on government reports are so indicated and copyright is claimed for those parts to the extent applicable to compilations of such works.

Independent verification should be sought for any data, advice or recommendations contained in this book. In addition, no responsibility is assumed by the publisher for any injury and/or damage to persons or property arising from any methods, products, instructions, ideas or otherwise contained in this publication.

This publication is designed to provide accurate and authoritative information with regard to the subject matter covered herein. It is sold with the clear understanding that the Publisher is not engaged in rendering legal or any other professional services. If legal or any other expert assistance is required, the services of a competent person should be sought. FROM A DECLARATION OF PARTICIPANTS JOINTLY ADOPTED BY A COMMITTEE OF THE AMERICAN BAR ASSOCIATION AND A COMMITTEE OF PUBLISHERS.

Additional color graphics may be available in the e-book version of this book.

Library of Congress Cataloging-in-Publication Data

ISBN: 978-1-62948-403-7

Published by Nova Science Publishers, Inc. † New York

CONTENTS

PREFACE

The psychological health of active duty servicemembers has been an issue of significant concern for Congress in recent years, with particular attention to the links between deployments and psychological health concerns, such as post-traumatic stress disorder (PTSD). News stories have emphasized the challenges faced by some servicemembers returning from deployments, but psychological health is a salient issue for the entire active duty force. Overall, mental health disorders have significant impacts on servicemember health care utilization, disability, and attrition from service. In 2011, mental disorders accounted for more hospitalizations of servicemembers than any other illness and more outpatient care than all illnesses except musculoskeletal injuries and routine medical care. This book will discuss the prevalence of different psychological health concerns within the Armed Forces, current mental health screening and treatments, and DOD responses. It will also provide an overview of the recommendations of key reports and studies, past congressional actions and funding, and current issues for Congress. Finally, the book discusses specific mental health issues, including PTSD, alcohol and drug use disorders, depressive disorders, traumatic brain injury, and suicide in more detail.

Chapter 1 – Report of a Congressional Research Service publication, on Post-Traumatic Stress Disorder and Other Mental Health Problems in the Military: Oversight Issues for Congress, dated August 8, 2013.

Chapter 2 – Report of the United States Government Accountability Office publication, Report to the Ranking Member, Subcommittee on Health, Committee on Veterans' Affairs, House of Representatives on VA Health Care: VA Spends Millions on Post-Traumatic Stress Disorder Research and Incorporates Research Outcomes into Guidelines and Policy for Post-Traumatic Stress Disorder Services, dated January 2011.

In: Post-Traumatic Stress and Mental Health ... ISBN: 978-1-62948-403-7
Editor: Jeffrey N. Lentz

Chapter 1

POST-TRAUMATIC STRESS DISORDER AND OTHER MENTAL HEALTH PROBLEMS IN THE MILITARY: OVERSIGHT ISSUES FOR CONGRESS*

Katherine Blakeley

SUMMARY

Military servicemembers suffering from post-traumatic stress disorder (PTSD), traumatic brain injury (TBI), and depression, as well as military suicides, continue to be a major concern of Congress. Numerous legislative provisions have been enacted over the past years to address these issues. Members will likely seek to offer legislation in the 113th Congress to address this complex set of issues.

This report is intended to provide assistance in understanding the issues associated with psychological health in the active duty forces, potential congressional responses, and what questions may remain unanswered.

Key points in this report include the following:

* This is an edited, reformatted and augmented version of a Congressional Research Service publication, CRS Report for Congress R43175, prepared for Members and Committees of Congress, from www.crs.gov, dated August 8, 2013.

- mental disorders such as PTSD are poorly understood and in most cases cannot be physically identified but, rather, must be diagnosed using symptoms reported by the servicemember;
- estimates of the prevalence of mental health conditions in any given population may be greatly affected by the methodology used;
- diagnoses of mental health conditions among active duty servicemembers have increased substantially relative to non-deployed servicemembers. This increase may be due to the psychological toll of exposure to conflict, but may also be due in part to increased and improved screening methods as well as Department of Defense (DOD) efforts to reduce the stigma associated with seeking mental health treatment that might dissuade some servicemembers from reporting mental health concerns or accessing care; and
- reliable evidence is lacking as to the quality of mental health care and counseling offered in DOD facilities. A 2012 Institute of Medicine (IOM) study recommended that DOD undertake efforts to measure the effectiveness of efforts to improve quality, such as training providers in evidence-based practice, that are not integrated into the system of mental health care offered in DOD treatment facilities.

Significant areas for potential congressional oversight activities regarding psychological health in the active duty forces include the following:

- research into the causes and physical manifestations of psychological health conditions, screening tools, and treatments;
- the effectiveness of screening and treatment efforts;
- servicemembers' access to mental health care, including efforts to reduce the stigma of seeking mental health care, waiting times for care, staffing levels of mental health treatment professionals, mental health care available in remote or deployed settings, and care available to de-activated Reserve and Guard members;
- the quality of mental health care available to servicemembers, including the use of appropriate and effective treatments by qualified mental health treatment professionals;
- oversight of ongoing program evaluation efforts, including evaluation of the variety of suicide-prevention, stigma-reduction, and transition assistance programs within the services and DOD; and
- the costs of mental health care for active duty servicemembers, including present costs through the Defense Health Program, as

well as the future costs of mental health care once servicemembers are no longer part of the active duty forces.

INTRODUCTION

The psychological health of active duty servicemembers has been an issue of significant concern for Congress in recent years, with particular attention to the links between deployments and psychological health concerns, such as post-traumatic stress disorder (PTSD). News stories have emphasized the challenges faced by some servicemembers returning from deployments, but psychological health is a salient issue for the entire active duty force. It should also be pointed out that mental health issues are not unique to servicemembers or military service. Research suggests that an estimated 26.2% of Americans ages 18 and older experience a diagnosable mental disorder in any given year.[1]

Within the Department of Defense (DOD), the Office of the Assistant Secretary of Defense (Health Affairs) is primarily responsible for the medical aspects of mental health issues. The individual military services (Army, Navy, Marine Corps, and Air Force) also conduct a variety of mental health programs and suicide prevention efforts. In 2012, a Defense Suicide Prevention Office was opened to provide suicide prevention services across all the services.

This report will discuss the prevalence of different psychological health concerns within the Armed Forces, current mental health screening and treatments, and DOD responses. It will also provide an overview of the recommendations of key reports and studies, past congressional actions and funding, and current issues for Congress. Finally, the report discusses specific mental health issues, including PTSD, alcohol and drug use disorders, depressive disorders, traumatic brain injury, and suicide in more detail.

Psychological Health in the Military

Mental Health Disorders, Including PTSD, Anxiety, and Depression

Overall, mental health disorders have significant impacts on servicemember health care utilization, disability, and attrition from service. In 2011, mental disorders accounted for more hospitalizations of servicemembers than any other illness and more outpatient care than all illnesses except musculoskeletal injuries and routine medical care.[2]

Between 2001 and 2011, the rate of mental health diagnoses among active duty servicemembers increased approximately 65%. A total of 936,283 servicemembers, or former servicemembers during their period of service, have been diagnosed with at least one mental disorder over this time period (see Figure 1).

Nearly 49% of these servicemembers were diagnosed with more than one mental disorder.[3]

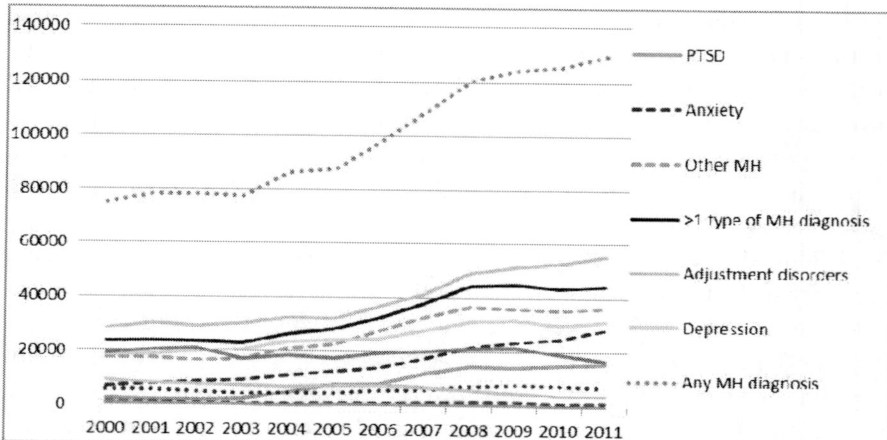

Source: Data provided by the Armed Forces Health Surveillance Center, and expended from the data presented in "Mental disorders and mental health problems, active component, U.S. Armed Forces, 2000-2011," Medical Surveillance Monthly Report, 19(6), June 2012.

Notes: An individual may be a case within a category only once per lifetime. This figure presents the number of diagnoses, not the incidence (rate of new diagnoses in a population) or prevalence (total number of cases in a population). As such, the number of diagnoses can be expected to change in relation to changes in the population size.

Figure 1. Number of Mental Disorder Diagnoses, 2000-2011.

Between 2000 and 2011, diagnoses of adjustment disorders, depression, and anxiety disorders (excluding PTSD) made up 26%, 17%, and 10% of all diagnoses of mental disorder diagnoses. Alcohol abuse and dependence disorders, and substance abuse and dependence disorders made up 13% and 4%, respectively.

PTSD represented approximately 6% of mental disorder diagnoses over this time period.[4] (See *Figure 2.*)

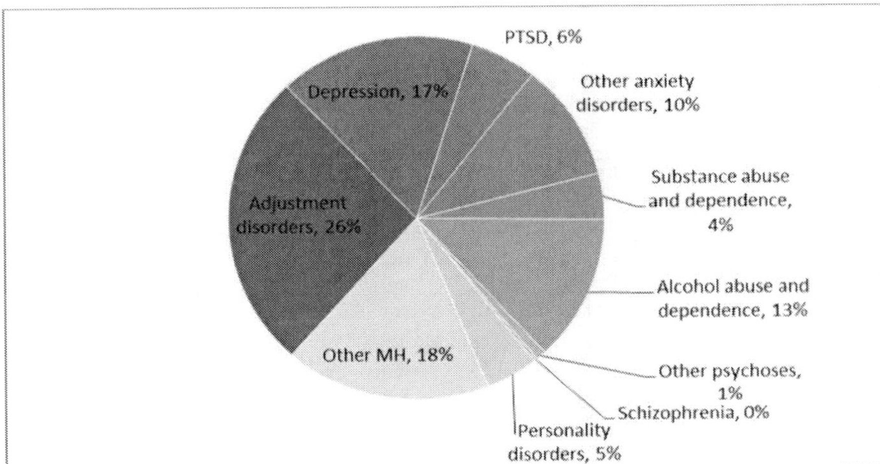

Source: Data provided by the Armed Forces Health Surveillance Center, extended from the data presented in "Mental disorders and mental health problems, active component, U.S. Armed Forces, 2000-2011," Medical Surveillance Monthly Report, 19(6), June 2012.

Figure 2. Diagnoses of Mental Disorders in the Active Duty Forces, 2000-2011.

The rates of specific mental disorders have also changed dramatically between 2000 and 2011. The reported incidence of PTSD has increased approximately 650%, from about 170 diagnoses per 100,000 person years in 2000, to approximately 1,110 diagnoses per 100,000 person years in 2011. The incidence of anxiety, adjustment disorders, and depression diagnoses has also increased. By contrast, the incidence of alcohol abuse/dependence, schizophrenia, and personality disorders fell. (See *Table 1, Figure 3.)*

Table 1. Reported Changes in Incidence Rates of Mental Disorder Diagnoses Between 2000-2011

Category of Mental Disorder Diagnosis	Change in Incidence Rate per 100,000 Person-Years
PTSD	656.5%
Anxiety	225.8%
Other MH	125.8%
Adjustment disorders	97.7%
Other psychoses	36.5%
Depression	62.4%
Substance abuse and dependence	28.5%

Table 1. (Continued)

Category of Mental Disorder Diagnosis	Change in Incidence Rate per 100,000 Person-Years
Alcohol abuse and dependence	-20.2%
Schizophrenia	-22.0%
Personality disorders	-50.0%
Any MH diagnosis	61.9%
More than one MH diagnosis	84.9%

Source: Analysis by CRS. Data provided by the Armed Forces Health Surveillance Center, expanded from the data presented in "Mental disorders and mental health problems, active component, U.S. Armed Forces, 2000- 2011." Medical Surveillance Monthly Report, 19(6), June 2012.

Notes: Incidence rate is number of diagnoses per 100,000 person-years. For example, for an incidence rate of 7,000, out of a population of 100,000 observed for one year, 7,000 new diagnoses would be expected. For a population of 50,000 observed for one year (50,000 person years), or a population of 100,000 observed for 6 months (also 50,000 person-years), 3,500 new diagnoses would be expected.

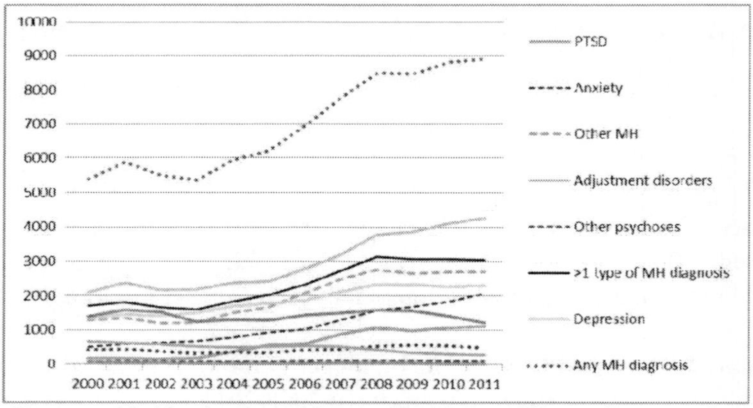

Source: Data provided by the Armed Forces Health Surveillance Center, and expanded form of the data presented in "Mental disorders and mental health problems, active component, U.S. Armed Forces, 2000-2011," Medical Surveillance Monthly Report, 19(6), June 2012.

Notes: Incidence rate is number of diagnoses per 100,000 person-years. For example, for an incidence rate of 7,000, out of a population of 100,000 observed for one year, 7,000 new diagnoses would be expected. For a population of 50,000 observed for one year (50,000 person years), 3,500 new diagnoses would be expected.

Figure 3. Incidence Rate of Mental Disorder Diagnoses, 2001-2011.

Among the services, the Army, followed by the Marine Corps, has consistently had the highest incidence rates for PTSD, major depression, alcohol dependence, and substance dependence between 2007 and 2010, followed by the Navy and the Air Force. (See *Figure 4.)*

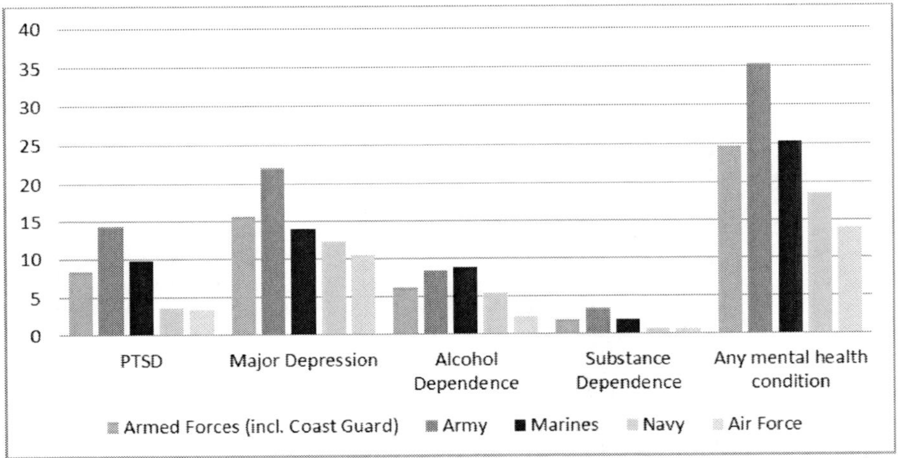

Source: Analysis by CRS. Data from "Selected mental disorders among active component members, U.S. Armed Forces, 2007-2010." Monthly Surveillance Medical Report, Armed Forces Health Surveillance Center, Vol. 17, No 11. Supplemental Report, p. 3.

Notes: Incident rates are cases per 1,000 persons per year. In each year from 2007 to 2010, the Army had the highest incidence rates of PTSD, major depression, substance dependence, and of mental health diagnoses in general. The Army was also the service with the highest incidence rate of alcohol dependence diagnoses in 2009 and 2010. In 2007 and 2008 the Marine Corps had the highest incidence rate of alcohol dependence.

Figure 4. Incidence Rate of Selected Mental Health Conditions by Service, 2010.

Hospitalizations for mental health mental disorders were steady between 2000 and 2006, before increasing more than 50% from 2006 through 2009, from 10,262 to 15,328. This increase in hospitalizations was driven by sharp increases in hospitalization for PTSD, depression, and substance abuse. Calculated by lost duty time, the Army has been the service most affected by hospitalizations of active duty servicemembers for mental disorders, followed by the Marine Corps. (See Figure 5.)

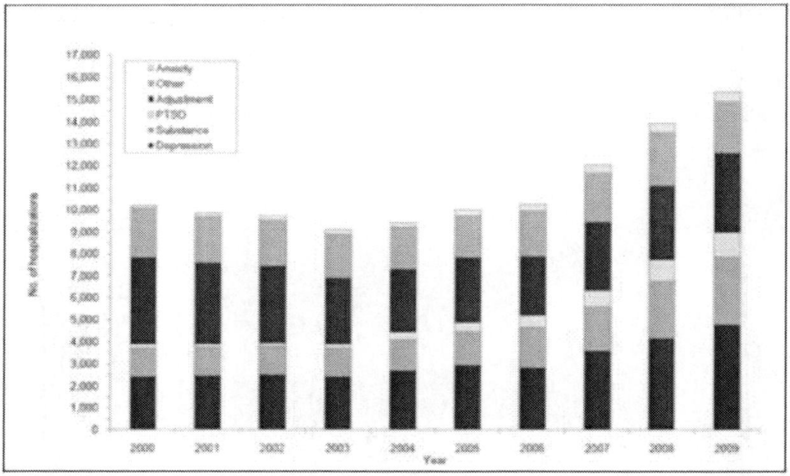

Source: From "Hospitalizations for mental disorders, active components, U.S. Armed Forces, January 2000- December 2009." Medical Surveillance Monthly Report, Vol. 17, No 11, November 2010, p. 10.

Figure 5. Hospitalizations for Mental Disorders. (Active Duty Forces, 2000-2009)

Table 2. Changes in Incidence Rates of DSM-IV "V Codes" Between 2000-2011

Category of Other Mental Health Problem	Change in Incidence Rate per 100,000 Person-Years
Mental, behavioral and substance abuse	117.8%
Family circumstance	-1.1%
Any V code	-19.2%
Life circumstance problem	-31.2%
Partner relationship	-31.2%
More than 1 type of V code	-38.4%
Maltreatment related	-79.1%

Source: Analysis by CRS. Data provided by the Armed Forces Health Surveillance Center, expanded from the data presented in "Mental disorders and mental health problems, active component, U.S. Armed Forces, 2000- 2011." Medical Surveillance Monthly Report, 19(6), June 2012.

Notes: Incidence rate is number of diagnoses per 100,000 person-years, for example, for an incidence rate of 7,000, out of a population of 100,000 observed for one year, 7,000 new diagnoses would be expected. For a population of 50,000 observed for one year (50,000 person years), or a population of 100,000 observed for 6 months (also 50,000 person-years), 3,500 new diagnoses would be expected.

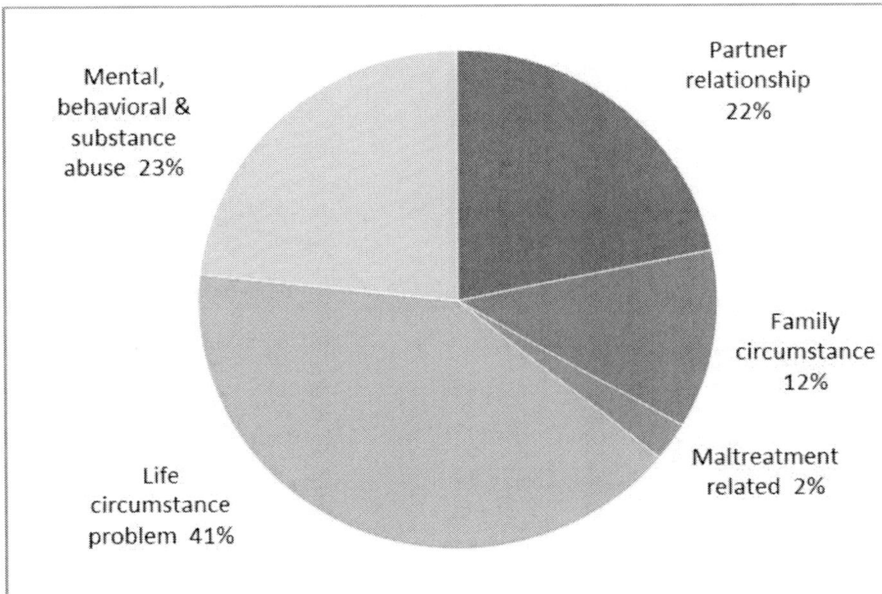

Source: Analysis by CRS. Data provided by the Armed Forces Health Surveillance Center, expanded from of the data presented in "Mental disorders and mental health problems, active component, U.S. Armed Forces, 2000-2011." Medical Surveillance Monthly Report, 19(6), June 2012.

Notes: The number of active duty members who sought treatment for other mental health problems in 2011 totaled nearly 32,000. These numbers do not include servicemembers who received a diagnosis for a specific mental disorder.

Figure 6. Other Mental Health Problems in the Active Duty Forces, 2011.

Traumatic Brain Injury (TBI)

TBI has been considered a "signature injury" of the conflicts in Iraq and Afghanistan. However, approximately 80% of servicemember TBIs occur in a non-deployed setting. Common causes of TBI include vehicle crashes, falls, sports and recreation activities, and military training.[5]

Since 2001, it is reported that servicemembers have experienced about 255,852 TBIs, including approximately 212,741 incidences of mild TBI, approximately 20,168 incidences of moderate TBI, approximately 6,472 incidences of severe TBI/penetrating head injuries, and 16,471 unclassifiable TBIs. Incidents of mild TBI rose sharply between 2005 and 2007, due in part to more aggressive screening measures for mild TBI instituted in 2006.[6] (See *Figure 7.)* Diagnoses of TBI in deployed settings nearly doubled between

2010 and 2011, due in part to a greater focus on identifying and treating TBIs among deployed servicemembers.[7]

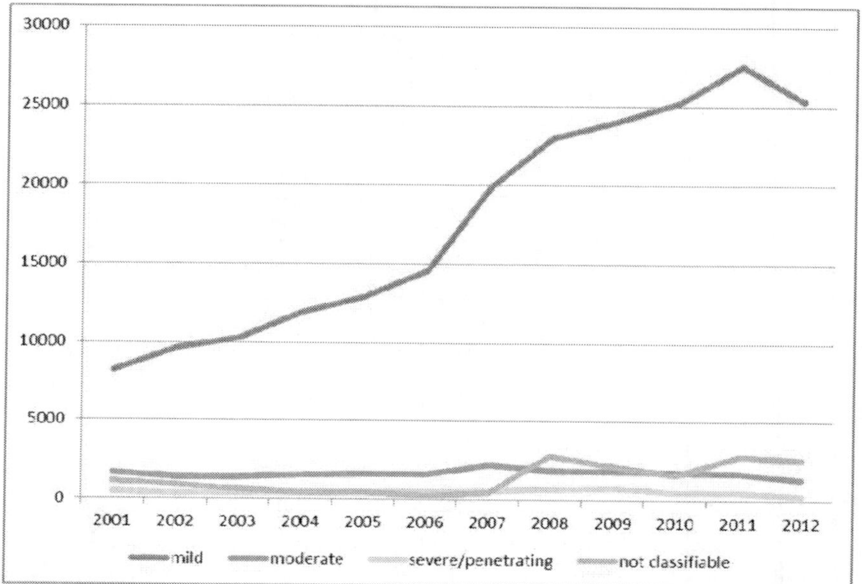

Source: Data provided by the Armed Forces Health Surveillance Center (AFHSC), April 2013.

Notes: The diagnosis and severity of injury were determined using ICD-9 codes. The ICD-9 codes are the International Statistical Classification of Diseases and Related Health Problems standard codes published by the World Health Organization to classify diseases and injuries, 9th Revision. Each data set is based on garrison medical encounters in the Defense Medical Surveillance System, Standard Ambulatory Data Records, Health Care Service Record and TRICARE Encounter Data feeds, and theater medical encounters in the Theater Medical Data Store. Servicemembers may be counted only once, at the most severe level of injury. Therefore, these data cannot track multiple TBIs experienced by the same servicemember.

These data include TBIs for active duty and activated Guard and Reserve members.

Figure 7. TBI Incidence by Severity, 2001-2012.

Suicide

Beginning in 2010, suicide has been the second-leading cause of death for active duty servicemembers, behind only war injuries.[8] Researchers have suggested that, similar to suicides among civilians, suicides by servicemembers are often impulsive acts triggered by various stressors, including relationship problems and financial or legal problems.[9]

Suicides among the active duty forces have increased between 1998 and 2012, rising from approximately 200 deaths by suicide in 1998 to 349 in 2012. Between 1998 and 2011, the incidence rate of deaths by suicide for active duty servicemembers overall was approximately 14 per 100,000 person years. Most of the increase in suicide rates between 2000 and 2011 has been concentrated in the Army and Marine Corps. Between 2005 and 2009, the incidence of suicide has nearly doubled for Army and Marine personnel, while remaining approximately level for Navy and Air Force personnel.[10] In 2011, the suicide rate for Army personnel was approximately 23 per 100,000, while the rates for the Navy and Marine Corps were approximately 15 per 100,000 and the rate for the Air Force was approximately 13 per 100,000.

While the rates of suicide in the Armed Forces overall have increased between 1998 and 2011, the rates for active duty servicemembers overall remain lower than for comparable civilian populations. Lower suicide rates among the Armed Forces have been attributed to a variety of factors, including the servicemember's full-time employment; "healthy-worker" effects, including a sense of belonging and purpose among active duty servicemembers; and universal access to health care among the military population.[11]

Screening and Treatment Programs

Screening

Accession Screening

Accession into the uniformed services provides an opportunity to screen potential servicemembers for potential behavioral health issues. Certain learning, behavioral, and psychological conditions are considered disqualifying for military service.[12] However, there is no required battery of psychological tests for accessions into the military other than the learning and behavioral questions on the Armed Services Vocational Aptitude Battery (ASVAB). During the course of the history and physical that every recruit is required to complete, specific questions and other methods are utilized to evoke potential markers of psychological and behavioral dysfunction potentially incompatible with military service.

Since 2009, the Supplemental Health Screening Questionnaire has augmented the standard Report of Medical History (DD 2807-2). This form includes 12 queries regarding past history of psychiatric, psychological, or behavioral issues as well as questions regarding substance abuse. Any condition reported or elucidated during the examination that does not meet the Department of Defense Instruction (DODI) 6130.03: Accession Medical Standard is considered disqualifying.

Each service has the authority to waive the standard on a case by case basis. According to data provided by DOD from the U.S. Military Entrance Processing Command's database, out of 296,000 accessions in fiscal year 2009, a total of 11,845 accessions with medical waivers were granted. Of these, 1,178 were accessions with mental health conditions, of which 127 were for anxiety, 32 for depression, 182 for personality disorder, and 19 for PTSD.[13]

In addition, during the physical examination portion of accession medical evaluation, evidence of self-harm, mutilation, or excessive or otherwise inappropriate tattooing or piercings, among other physical findings, would lead the examiner to evaluate the recruit further for psychological problems or maladaptive behavior.

In any of the above situations, reasonable suspicion on the part of the examiner that the recruit may manifest psychological or behavior health conditions incompatible with service would be referred for further psychological evaluation and if found unfit, would be subjected to the decision of the individual service to exercise its waiver authority.

The study of the effects of prior psychological and behavioral health issues on successful military service is ongoing. Multiple forms of additional screening tools have and are being piloted, however, to date, the requisite data to determine if these tools have any predictive value in determining the ability of a recruit to complete a successful tour of duty are still outstanding.

Periodic Health Assessment—Annual Physical

Servicemembers are required to receive an annual physical examination known as a periodic health assessment (PHA). The PHA is intended to identify changes in health status, including mental health changes, especially those that could impact a member's ability to perform military duties.[14]

Pre-Deployment and Post-Deployment Mental Health Assessments and Reassessments

Servicemembers who are deployed in connection with a contingency operation are required to receive face-to-face mental health assessments conducted by mental health professionals. Separate assessments are required at four separate times: within 120 days before the estimated date of deployment, between 90 and 180 days after return from deployment, between 181 days and 18 months after return from deployment, and between 18 and 30 months after return from deployment. Assessments must be administered at least 90 days apart.[15]

Deployment Limiting Conditions

The following conditions are cited as limiting deployability, meaning an individual diagnosed with these conditions may not deploy:

1) Psychotic and/or bipolar disorders;
2) Psychiatric disorders under treatment with fewer than 3 months of demonstrated stability;
3) Clinical psychiatric disorders with residual symptoms that impair duty performance;
4) Mental health conditions that pose a substantial risk for deterioration and/or recurrence of impairing symptoms in the deployed environment; and
5) Chronic medical conditions that require ongoing treatment with antipsychotics, lithium, or anticonvulsants.[16]

Treatment Programs

Servicemembers on active duty are covered by DOD's TRICARE Prime health insurance program. Under this program servicemembers receive free health care without any copayments, deductibles, or premiums. Servicemembers typically receive most of their health care in a military treatment facility but may be referred to private providers for specialty care or if insufficient providers are available on base.

Prior authorization is not required for services received through a military treatment facility but is required for all nonemergency inpatient behavioral health care services. Psychiatric emergencies do not require prior authorization, but authorization is required for continued stay in the facility beyond the initial emergency.

The Telemental Health program is available to all U.S. TRICARE beneficiaries. At Telemental Health-participating TRICARE facilities, secure audio-visual conferencing is available to connect with off-site mental health care providers.

TRICARE covers medical treatments that DOD has deemed to be proven safe and effective by reliable evidence as defined in regulation.[17] TRICARE excludes from coverage services and supplies that are not medically or psychologically necessary for the diagnosis or treatment of a covered illness (including mental disorder) or injury. It also excludes treatments that are not proven medically. All services related to a non-covered condition or treatment, or provided by an unauthorized provider, are also excluded from coverage. Authorized providers of mental health care include psychiatrists, clinical psychologists, certified marriage and family therapists, certified nurse practitioners, and certified clinical social workers. Certain services otherwise not covered by TRICARE may, in certain circumstances, be provided through the DOD Supplemental Health Care Program.[18] This program is not subject to the statutory TRICARE coverage limitations and has been used, for example, to provide cognitive therapy to TBI patients.

Mental Health Providers

Active duty servicemembers may receive treatment from military mental health providers as well as federal civilian and contractor mental health providers. In some circumstances active duty servicemembers also may be referred outside of military treatment facilities to private providers. Mental health providers include psychiatrists, psychologists, social workers, licensed mental health counselors, and psychiatric nurse practitioners. Concerns about the potential for servicemembers to lack appropriate access to mental health care due to insufficient numbers of mental health providers led to legislation mandating that DOD develop and implement a plan to significantly increase the number of DOD military and civilian mental health personnel by September 30, 2013.[19] Overall, Defense Health Program personnel has increased, with officer end strength growing from 31,244 in fiscal year 2012 to a projected 31,852 for fiscal year 2014 and from 64,236 civilian personnel to 67,577 over the same period.

The 2014 budget request specifically includes an increase of $21 million to fund expansion of embedded behavioral health (EBH) teams in the Army to 19 Army installations world-wide. EBH teams are composed of 13 civilian behavioral health personnel and provide behavioral health care to servicemembers in close proximity to their unit areas. The intent is to optimize care and maximize behavioral health resources through early identification of servicemembers with behavioral health problems.[20]

Clinical Practice Guidelines

Treatment of servicemembers is generally provided by either civilian or military mental health care providers working in a military treatment facility. Their treatment decisions typically are made following clinical practice guidelines. DOD and the Department of Veterans Affairs (VA) have worked together to develop joint clinical practice guidelines, including, among others, guidelines for PTSD,[21] TBI,[22] depression,[23] and substance abuse disorder.[24]

The VA/DOD Evidence-Based Practice Guideline Work Group (EBPWG) was established to advise the VA/DOD Health Executive Council on the use of clinical and epidemiological evidence to improve the health of the population across the Veterans Health Administration (VHA) and Military Health System. The EBPWG has two co-chairpersons (one from VA and one from DOD) and includes representatives for each military branch and the VHA Veterans Integrated Service Networks (VISN). The workgroup was first chartered in 2004. It continues to refine existing guidelines as circumstances require and develop new clinical practice guidelines.

Stigma Reduction Efforts

Concern has been expressed that servicemembers may underreport mental health conditions as a result of stigma attached to seeking treatment for those conditions. DOD has issued instructions to all heads of DOD components stating:

It is DOD policy that:

a) The DOD shall foster a culture of support in the provision of mental health care and voluntarily sought substance abuse education to military personnel in order to dispel the stigma of seeking mental health care and/or substance misuse education services.
b) Healthcare providers shall follow a presumption that they are not to notify a Service member's commander when the Service member obtains mental health care or substance abuse education services.[25]

This policy further requires that "Commanders must also reduce stigma through positive regard for those who seek mental health assistance to restore and maintain their mission readiness, just as they would view someone seeking treatment for any other medical issue."

Efforts to address the stigma issue may be, at least in part, responsible for greater rates of mental health diagnoses. The Armed Forces Health Surveillance Center stated that:

> The Department of Defense has made significant efforts to reduce stigmas associated with care seeking for, and treatment of, mental illnesses and to remove barriers to receiving timely and appropriate diagnostic and treatment services. Undoubtedly, such changes have resulted in increases in the detection and treatment of previously undiagnosed mental disorders and more complete documentation of mental disorders in electronic medical records.[26]

Nevertheless, the Mental Health Advisory Teams report a stable response pattern over the years among junior enlisted servicemembers to questions regarding factors that affect an individual's decision to receive mental health services, with over 30% of individuals screening positive for mental disorders reporting fear of harm to career.[27]

Costs of Mental Disorder Treatment

Many active duty servicemembers and activated Guard and Reserve members seek mental disorder treatment through the military health care system.

Between FY2007 and FY2012, the costs to the military health system of providing mental disorder treatments to active duty servicemembers and activated Guard and Reserve members has nearly doubled, increasing from about $468 million in FY2007 to about $994 million in FY2012. (See *Figure 8*.) These numbers include mental disorder treatment costs for all active duty and activated Guard and Reserve members. Costs for mental disorder treatments for servicemembers while deployed are not available.

In FY2012, the military medical system spent nearly $1 billion on mental disorder treatment costs for active duty and activated Guard and Reserve members. Over half of these costs, about $567 million, were for outpatient active duty mental health treatments. Overall, approximately 63% of mental disorder treatment costs were for outpatient treatment, 31% for in-patient treatment, and 7% for pharmacy costs.

Mental disorder treatment for active duty servicemembers accounted for 89% of military health care spending on mental disorder treatment between FY2007 and FY2012, approximately $4 billion.

Over the same time frame, the military health system spent about $461 million on mental health care treatment for activated Guard and Reserve members. (See *Figure 9*.)

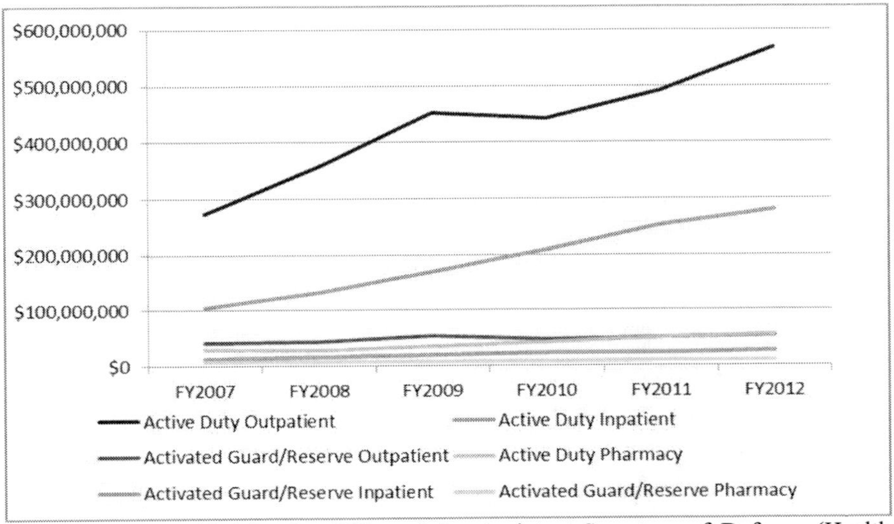

Source: Data provided by the Office of the Assistant Secretary of Defense (Health Affairs), January 30, 2012.

Notes: Includes total cost of inpatient, outpatient, and pharmacy records as of January 22, 2013. FY2012 data are estimated to completion. Not all of the records for FY2012 have been received, therefore an estimate, with a high level of confidence, is provided.

Not all costs of active duty and activated Reserve and Guard mental health treatment will appear in this chart, as not all servicemembers seek mental disorder treatment through the military health system. Deactivated Guard and Reserve members are covered by the Transitional Assistance Management Program for 180 days. Following this 180 days, deactivated Guard and Reserve members may be eligible to purchase TRICARE Reserve Select coverage. Those ineligible to purchase TRICARE Reserve Select may be eligible to purchase the Continued Health Care Benefit Program, which can provide benefits for up to 18 or 36 months, depending on eligibility.

Figure 8. Costs of Military Mental Disorder Treatment for Active Duty and Activated Guard/Reserve. (FY2007-FY2012, in millions of $)

Not all costs of active duty and activated Reserve and Guard mental health treatment will appear in this chart, as not all servicemembers seek mental disorder treatment through the military health system. Deactivated Guard and Reserve members are covered by the Transitional Assistance Management Program for 180 days. Following this 180 days, deactivated Guard and Reserve members may be eligible to purchase TRICARE Reserve Select coverage. Those ineligible to purchase TRICARE Reserve Select may be eligible to purchase the Continued Health Care Benefit Program, which can provide benefits for up to 18 or 36 months, depending on eligibility.

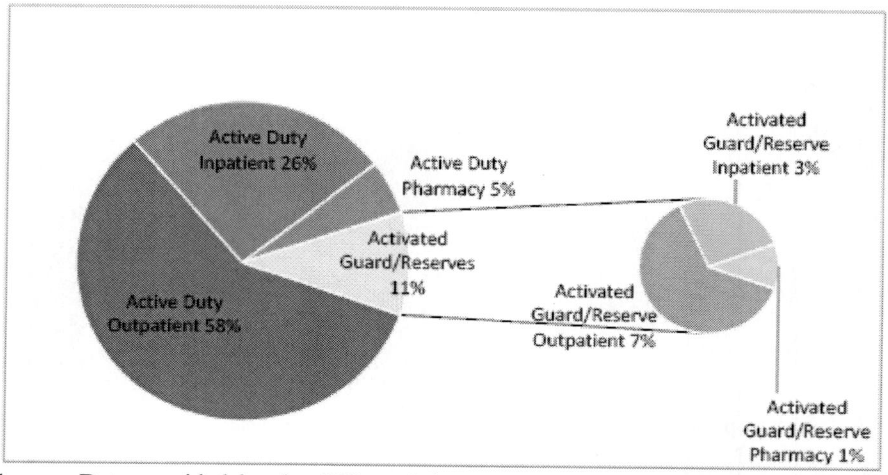

Source: Data provided by the Office of the Assistant Secretary of Defense (Health Affairs), January 30, 2012.

Notes: Includes total cost of inpatient, outpatient, and pharmacy records as of January 22, 2013. FY2012 data are estimated to completion. Not all of the records for FY2012 have been received, therefore an estimate, with a high level of confidence, is provided.

Figure 9. Active Duty and Activated Guard/Reserve Mental Disorder Treatment Costs, FY2012.

Other Responses

Prevention Programs

DOD and the services have implemented a number of programs and strategies to promote psychological resilience among servicemembers.[28] "Psychological resilience" is understood to be the ability to bounce back from negative experiences. It is thought to be related to an individual's ability to avoid experiencing diagnosable mental health conditions. However, a RAND study reported that "there is very little empirical evidence that these programs effectively build resilience."[29]

With respect to suicide, "DOD and each service have a myriad of activities currently in place to prevent suicides."[30] To better coordinate these efforts, DOD has created a Defense Suicide Prevention Office to oversee cross-service programs. These programs include (1) a DOD Suicide Prevention and Risk Reduction Committee that meets monthly, (2) the Real Warriors Campaign, a public education initiative to address the stigma of seeking psychological care and treatment, (3) the Department of Defense Suicide Event Report (DoDSER), and (4) annual suicide-prevention conferences. In addition, the services each have a suicide prevention program manager to oversee service-specific programs. However, here too empirical evidence for the efficacy of these programs is limited. One recent study stated that the "quality of mental health care and counseling offered in DOD is unknown, and efforts to improve quality, such as training providers in evidence-based practice, are not integrated into the system of mental health care offered in DOD treatment facilities."[31]

Defense Centers of Excellence for Psychological Health and Traumatic Brain Injury

The Defense Centers of Excellence for Psychological Health and Traumatic Brain Injury (DCOE) was established in 2007 to focus on prevention, outreach, and care for servicemembers with psychological health conditions, including TBI. The DCOE for Psychological Health and Traumatic Brain Injury are intended to be principal integrators and authorities on psychological health and traumatic brain injury knowledge and standards for DOD. There are three centers under the DCOE: the Defense and Veterans Brain Injury Center, the Deployment Health Clinical Center, and the National Center for Telehealth and Technology. Support responsibility for DCOE is currently shifting from the TRICARE Management Activity office to the Army's Medical Research and Materiel Command. A key project of the DCOE centers in 2013 will be "determining the impact of mental health programs across the military."[32]

PAST RECOMMENDATIONS AND ACTIONS

Reports, Studies, and Recommendations

A number of reports have made recommendations that Congress could build upon in fashioning legislation or conducting oversight. These reports include in reverse chronological order:

Institute of Medicine

The Institute of Medicine (IOM) published the results of the first phase of a two-part study titled "Treatment for Posttraumatic Stress Disorder (PTSD) in Military and Veteran Populations" in July 2012.[33] The IOM report concluded with seven general recommendations, in five major areas, for further areas of research and service. The report findings were summarized by the DOD as:

- *History, Diagnostic Criteria, and Epidemiology*—Servicemembers that served in OEF/OIF/OND appear to have a 13%-20% lifetime prevalence of PTSD. In contrast, the unadjusted general population lifetime prevalence of PTSD in adults appears to be 8%;
- *Neurobiology*—Further research is needed to identify biomarkers of PTSD, brain imaging diagnostic models, and effective pharmacologic agents to enhance therapy-related learning;
- *Programs and Services for PTSD in the DOD and VA*—Both the DOD and VA have a played an active and pivotal role in the prevention, screening, diagnosis, and treatment of PTSD; however, further evaluation is needed to identify the effectiveness of these efforts;
- *Prevention*—DOD supports several PTSD prevention programs that build resiliency and teach servicemembers to anticipate some of the traumatic events commonly experienced in combat zones;
- *Screening and Diagnosis*—Screening measures for PTSD are essential to the identification of servicemembers and veterans that need treatment. DOD currently utilizes screening tools, but needs to ensure that every servicemember identified through such screening methods is referred to trained professionals that can provide comprehensive assessments, diagnosis, and treatment;
- *Treatment*—The VA/DOD clinical practice guidelines for the management of PTSD make specific suggestions concerning treatment of PTSD symptoms. IOM recognizes that DOD offers numerous treatments for PTSD, and continues to develop additional treatment methods; and
- *Co-occurring Psychiatric and Medical Conditions and Psychosocial Complexities*—Given the presence of co-occurring conditions in more than 50% of OEF/OIF/OND veterans, IOM recommends evidence-based PTSD models to ensure the success of PTSD treatment for comorbid conditions.[34]

DOD generally concurred with the IOM report recommendations and findings. In Phase 2 of its study, the IOM will analyze barriers to care and ways to improve access to high-quality care for servicemembers and veterans.

RAND National Defense Research Institute

The RAND National Defense Research Institute released a study entitled "The War Within, Preventing Suicide in the U.S. Military" in February 2011. The War Within report made 14 recommendations in 6 categories:

1) Raise Awareness and Promote Self-Care;
2) Identify Those at High Risk;
3) Facilitate Access to High-Quality Care;
4) Provide High-Quality Care;
5) Restrict Access to Lethal Means; and
6) Respond Appropriately.[35]

DOD Task Force on the Prevention of Suicide

Section 733 of the Duncan Hunter National Defense Authorization Act for Fiscal Year 2009 (P.L. 110-417) required the Secretary of Defense to establish a Task Force "to examine matters relating to prevention of suicide by members of the Armed Forces." The DOD Task Force on the Prevention of Suicide by Members of the Armed Forces was established in August 2009, and was composed of seven DOD and seven non-DOD members. In August 2010, the Task Force issued a document entitled "The Challenge and the Promise: Strengthening the Force, Preventing Suicide and Saving Lives" that listed 49 findings and 76 associated recommendations. The Task Force's report did not address the earlier Army report described below. The findings fall into four areas: Organization and Leadership; Wellness Enhancement and Training; Access to, and Delivery of, Quality Care; and Surveillance, Investigations, and Research.[36]

Army Health Promotion, Risk Reduction, and Suicide Prevention

In July 2010, the Department of the Army issued a document entitled "Health Promotion, Risk Reduction, and Suicide Prevention (HP/RR/SP) Report" (hereinafter referred to as "the Army Report") that listed 67 specific conclusions and recommendations. Among the Army Report's major findings was discovering gaps in the identification and mitigation of high-risk behavior among soldiers. The report attributed these gaps to an operational tempo that required leadership focus on deployment rather than the enforcement of policies designed to ensure good order and discipline. The Army Report's recommendations were addressed to specific audiences, including Army Headquarters (HQDA), the Medical Command (MEDCOM), and Unit Commanders and are organized by themes. Recommendations addressed to HQDA appear most amenable to congressional action.

Mental Health Advisory Team Reports

Since 2003, DOD has deployed a series of teams to Iraq and Afghanistan to evaluate soldiers' psychological health in theater, the results of which are published as publicly available reports.[37] The sixth, and most recent, of these Mental Health Advisory Teams (MHAT VI) to report worked in Iraq from February to March 2009 and in Afghanistan from April to June 2009. The teams included research psychologists, a social worker, a psychiatric nurse, and enlisted behavioral-health specialists. The reports have made numerous recommendations, including to continue the "funding of basic-research models of concussive and traumatic brain injury work to advance the development of novel evidence-based interventions" that would require continuing congressional action in the form of appropriations.[38]

Executive Order 13625

Executive Order 13625, "Improving Access to Mental Health Services for Veterans, Service Members, and Military Families," issued on August 31, 2012, contained a number of provisions designed to increase access to and the quality of mental health care for active duty servicemembers, including establishing an interagency task force with an annual reporting requirement as well as providing for increased mental health care staffing within the Department of Veterans Affairs. With respect to broadly applicable issues, Executive Order 13625 provides for a National Research Action Plan, stating:

> Sec. 5. Improved Research and Development. (a) The lack of full understanding of the underlying mechanisms of PostTraumatic Stress Disorder (PTSD), other mental health conditions, and Traumatic Brain Injury (TBI) has hampered progress in prevention, diagnosis, and treatment. In order to improve the coordination of agency research into these conditions and reduce the number of affected men and women through better prevention, diagnosis, and treatment, the Departments of Defense, Veterans Affairs, Health and Human Services, and Education, in

coordination with the Office of Science and Technology Policy, shall establish a National Research Action Plan within 8 months of the date of this order.

(b) The National Research Action Plan shall include strategies to establish surrogate and clinically actionable biomarkers for early diagnosis and treatment effectiveness; develop improved diagnostic criteria for TBI; enhance our understanding of the mechanisms responsible for PTSD, related injuries, and neurological disorders following TBI; foster development of new treatments for these conditions based on a better understanding of the underlying mechanisms; improve data sharing between agencies and academic and industry researchers to accelerate progress and reduce redundant efforts without compromising privacy; and make better use of electronic health records to gain insight into the risk and mitigation of PTSD, TBI, and related injuries. In addition, the National Research Action Plan shall include strategies to support collaborative research to address suicide prevention.

(c) The Departments of Defense and Health and Human Services shall engage in a comprehensive longitudinal mental health study with an emphasis on PTSD, TBI, and related injuries to develop better prevention, diagnosis, and treatment options. Agencies shall continue ongoing collaborative research efforts, with an aim to enroll at least 100,000 service members by December 31, 2012, and include a plan for long term follow up with enrollees through a coordinated effort with the Department of Veterans Affairs.[39]

Previous Congressional Actions

Previous Congressional Funding

In addition to funding via the Defense Health Program, Congress has also allocated significant funding to research in these issues through the Congressionally-Directed Research Program.

There are no specific line items in the DOD budget request for suicide prevention or PTSD. Generally PTSD treatment and research costs are included in the Defense Health Program operations and maintenance (O&M) appropriation. Suicide prevention funds are included in the services' management accounts. Therefore, it is not possible to provide complete totals for all funding that may be directed to these purposes.

Table 3. Funding for Psychological Health (including PTSD and TBI) in millions

	FY2007/2008	*FY2009*	*FY2010*	*FY2011*	*FY2012*
O&M Funding	$454.5	$575.0	$655.9	$669.2	
RDT&E Funding	$506.1	$163.1	$230.3	$112.6	
Procurement Funding	$18.9	$20.0	$0	$0	
Defense O&M and Veterans' Brain	unknown	$34.25	$36.62	$38.38	$32.59
Injury Procurement	unknown	$1.7	$0	$0	$0
Center					
(DVBIC)					

The Congressionally Directed Medical Research Programs' Psychological Health and Traumatic Brain Injury (PH/TBI) Research Program (formerly called Post Traumatic Stress Disorder and Traumatic Brain Injury Research Program) was established in 2007 in response to U.S. Troop Readiness, Veterans' Care, Katrina Recovery, and Iraq Accountability Appropriations Act, P.L. 110-28, which provided $150 million (M) for research on PTSD and $150M for research on TBI. An additional $1M was provided for research on PTSD in P.L. 109-289.

Table 4. Funds Allocated for Psychological Health, FY2007-FY2013

Fiscal Year	Amount	Topic	Funding Language	Law
2013 (proposed)	$125 m (House) $60 m (Senate)	TBI and psychological health (proposed—CDMR)	H.Rept. 112-493 S.Rept. 112-196	Department of Defense Appropriations Act, 2013 (P.L. 113-6, 3/26/13)
2012	$10m	suicide prevention	H.Rept. 112-331 accompanying H.R. 2055	Consolidated Appropriations Act, 2012 (P.L. 112-74, 12/23/11)
2012	$135.5 m	TBI and psychological health (CDMR)	H.Rept. 112-331	Consolidated Appropriations Act, 2012 (P.L. 112-74, 12/23/11)
2011	$100 m	TBI and	House Rules	An Act To extend the

Fiscal Year	Amount	Topic	Funding Language	Law
		psychological health (CDMR)	Committee's tables accompanying H.R. 1473	Generalized System of Preferences, and for other purposes. (P.L. 112-40, 10/21/11)
2010	$120 m	TBI and psychological health (CDMR)	Joint Explanatory Statement to the Defense Appropriations Act , See Congressional Record, December 16, 2009, pp. H15319-H15320.	Department of Defense Appropriations Act, 2010 (P.L. 111-118, 12/19/09)
2009	$75 m	TBI and psychological health peer-reviewed research	H.Rept. 111-151. Allocates this funding per recommendations in H.Rept. 111-105 H.Rept. 111-105	Supplemental Appropriations Act, 2009 (P.L. 111-32, 6/24/09)
2009	$165 m	TBI and psychological health peer-reviewed research (CDMR)	See Congressional Record, September 24, 2008, pp. H9725 – H9726.	Consolidated Security, Disaster Assistance, and Continuing Appropriations Act, 2009 - Division C, Department of Defense Appropriations Act, 2009 (P.L. 110-329, 9/30/08)
2009	$190m	TBI and psychological health ($60m in Consolidated Health Care, $36m in Information Management/IT, $1m in Management Headquarters, $3m in Base Operation and Communication, $90m under Research and development)	H. Appropriations Committee Print, H.R. 2638	Consolidated Security, Disaster Assistance, and Continuing Appropriations Act, 2009 - Division C, Department of Defense Appropriations Act, 2009 (P.L. 110-329, 9/30/08)

Table 4. (Continued)

Fiscal Year	Amount	Topic	Funding Language	Law
2008	n/a	TBI and psychological health	P.L. 110-116 permits the $600m appropriated by P.L. 110-28 to be used for psychological health in addition to PTSD	Department of Defense Appropriations Act, 2008 (P.L. 110-116, 11/13/2007)
2007	$150m	TBI and psychological health (CDMR)	H.Rept. 109-676	Department of Defense Appropriations Act, 2007 (P.L. 109-289, 9/29/06)
2007	$151	PTSD (CDMR)	H.Rept. 109-676	Department of Defense Appropriations Act, 2007 (P.L. 109-289, 9/29/06).
2007	$600m	Treatment of TBI and PTSD ($118m for procurement, and $331.7m for RDT&E)	P.L. 110-28 pp. 134-135	U.S. Troop Readiness, Veterans' Care, Katrina Recovery, and Iraq Accountability Appropriations Act, 2007 (P.L. 110-28, 5/25/2007)

ISSUES FOR CONGRESS

As discussed elsewhere in the report and as listed in *Appendix B,* numerous laws have been enacted with provisions intended to address military mental health issues. These efforts include provisions to improve screening for mental health conditions and TBI, and providing for additional mental health providers, improved reporting, and continued research. While Congress has taken significant interest in issues related to the psychological health of the active duty forces, including PTSD, alcohol and substance abuse, depression, traumatic brain injury, and other mental health concerns, significant areas for potential congressional oversight remain. These include:

Research

The physical manifestations in the brain of mental health conditions, including PTSD, are poorly understood. Further research is needed to identify biomarkers, brain imaging, diagnostic models, and effective pharmacologic agents to enhance therapy-related learning. In conducting its oversight activities, Congress may wish to monitor ongoing research efforts for significant findings with implications for current mental health strategies, as well as consider whether there are gaps in research being conducted into the causes, biomarkers, and translational research for improved treatments.

Treatment

Screening measures for mental health conditions and TBI are essential to the identification of servicemembers and veterans that need treatment. DOD uses screening tools, but many observers recommend greater involvement of primary care providers in this process. Once servicemembers are identified as having potential diagnoses, oversight may be needed to assure they will be referred to trained professionals that can provide comprehensive assessments, diagnosis, and evidence-based treatment. Given the presence of co-occurring conditions in more than 50% of OEF/OIF/OND veterans, the IOM has recommended evidence-based models to ensure the success of treatments for comorbid conditions.[40] In conducting its oversight activities, Congress may wish to consider how the efficacy of treatment is monitored and evaluated.

Access to Care

Although Congress has provided resources allowing DOD to expand its pool of military mental health providers, Congress may wish to determine how DOD is responding to Institute of Medicine (IOM) findings expressing "serious misgivings about inadequate and untimely clinical follow-up and low rates of delivery of evidence based treatments, especially therapies to treat PTSD, depression, and substance use disorder. There are scant data documenting which treatments patients receive or whether those treatments were appropriate and timely."[41] Congress may also wish to examine the question of whether DOD is ensuring optimal means of access to and assignment of mental health care providers. Congress may also wish to examine the effectiveness of DOD initiatives to encourage servicemembers to seek care, and reduce the stigma of seeking mental health care.

Suicide Prevention

Congress may wish to examine the appropriateness of DOD's response to RAND study findings that the two most evidence-supported suicide prevention strategies are (1) training primary care physicians to assess servicemembers for depression or other risk factors for suicide, and (2) restricting servicemembers' access to lethal means, primarily private firearms.

Oversight

As discussed above, Executive Order 16325 requires a special interagency task force to evaluate:

- agency efforts to improve care quality and ensure that DOD and VA providers and community based mental health providers are trained in the most current evidence based methodologies for treating PTSD, TBI, depression, related mental health conditions, and substance abuse;
- agency efforts to improve awareness and reduce stigma for those needing to seek care; and
- agency research efforts to improve the prevention, diagnosis, and treatment of TBI, PTSD, and related injuries, and explore the need for an external research portfolio review.

Congress may wish to be apprised of these evaluation efforts.

In addition, Congress may consider whether additional oversight is necessary in areas such as:

- The allocation of resources between research, treatment, oversight, types of providers, provider to program staffing; and
- The efficacy of entities such as the DCOE for Psychological Health and Traumatic Brain Injury.

Costs of Mental Health Care Treatment

DOD's spending on mental health care treatment has increased, as the number of active duty servicemembers receiving diagnoses of mental health conditions and seeking treatment for these conditions has increased. Congress may wish to examine the role of supplying larger amounts of mental health care in the context of the Defense Health Program (DHP) appropriation since growth in the unified medical budget relative to the overall Defense budget has been identified by some senior leaders as unsustainable. Although this report has addressed only the issues of active duty mental health, Congress may well be interested in examining the implications of DOD's programs as they relate to the long-term costs experienced in the various programs administered by the VA.

Psychological Health in the Active Duty Forces

Within the active duty forces, psychological health issues include diagnosed mental disorders, such as depression or PTSD, as well as other mental health problems, such as problems with personal relationships or family circumstances. Other mental health issues facing the Armed Forces include traumatic brain injuries (TBI) and the suicides of servicemembers. Mental health issues in the active duty force have an impact not only on the individual servicemembers and their families, but also on the services as a whole.

Data Caveats

In this report, much of the data comes from past issues of the *Medical Surveillance Monthly Report*, a publication of DOD's Armed Forces Health Surveillance Center. The Armed Forces Health Surveillance Center (AFHSC) data include diagnoses received by servicemembers though the military medical system while on active duty service. The AFHSC data are the most complete and reliable data on servicemember diagnoses of mental health conditions, however, they likely represent the lower bound of actual servicemember incidences of diagnosable mental health disorders.

These data do not include servicemembers who may experience mental health problems but who do not seek treatment for them at a fixed military medical or reimbursable civilian location. Accordingly, these data likely underestimate the true incidence and prevalence numbers and rates among active duty servicemembers of the U.S. Armed Forces. Additionally, these data will likely not capture Reserve and Guard servicemembers who seek mental health treatment after they are deactivated.[42]

The underlying database used by the Armed Forces Health Surveillance Center is the Defense Medical Surveillance System. This database includes ambulatory visits and hospitalizations at fixed military medical and reimbursed civilian locations by servicemembers while on active duty, but does not include medical encounters at non-fixed locations. Medical encounters outside of fixed locations, such as care received in deployed settings or shipboard, are not routinely entered into the Defense Medical Surveillance System, and are thus not available for analysis.

These Armed Forces Health Surveillance Center data are of diagnoses of selected mental disorders, rather than continued care for diagnosed mental disorders. Incidence cases were generally defined as one hospitalization, two outpatient visits for the same diagnostic coding within 180 days, or a single outpatient visit in a psychiatric or mental health care specialty setting where the mental disorder was the primary or second diagnosis. Diagnostic codes of the selected mental disorders used to assemble the data are included in *Appendix A.* A servicemember was counted only once for each mental disorder during the surveillance period, although they may have been counted as a unique case for more than one of the mental disorders. Since many individuals have more than one diagnosis, the total of the number of diagnoses does not reflect the actual number of individual servicemembers who have been diagnosed.[43]

In considering relative numbers of diagnoses over time, it may also be useful to keep in mind that although there were 1,425,113 active duty servicemembers as of September 31, 2011[44] (at the end date of most of the time series data presented), over fiscal years 2001 through 2011, the total number of individuals who left military service since September 11, 2001, is estimated to be 1,790,290.

The methodology used by the Armed Forces Health Surveillance Center is different from that used in other studies frequently reported in the news media and elsewhere, therefore the results are not directly comparable. Data caveats may apply to other studies as well and in many instances may be discussed in the article or study itself. (Please see text box below for an explanation.)

Methodological Differences Between Monthly Medical Surveillance Report prevalence figures and other reported rates

"The news media have extensively covered the subject of mental health among military service members. Journalists have cited published numerical estimates of the frequency of mental health disorders in service members, especially among those who have deployed in support of current operations. The sources of such estimates have used differing methods and assumptions in collecting and analyzing their data. Accordingly, the rates of mental health disorders reported here are likely not directly comparable to other published rates. For example, the 2009 post-traumatic stress disorder (PTSD) incidence rate of 9.2 per 1,000 person-years and the prevalence rate of 1.9% among all service members of the active component contrast sharply with figures in media reports and the scientific literature. By way of illustration, news media have cited published medical articles that suggest PTSD prevalence of 12% or higher among service members following deployment.

Several important factors distinguish the results in this report from those in others. First, the results presented here reflect healthcare provider-assigned clinical diagnostic codes entered into the electronic medical records of service members, i.e., the providers rendered formal diagnoses of the conditions enumerated in this report. In contrast, other published studies have relied upon self-reported data from deployment health assessments, anonymous questionnaires, or retrospective interviews in which service members affirm or deny the presence of symptoms that are often associated with the mental health disorders of interest. ..."

From the Armed Forces Health Surveillance Center's *Monthly Medical Surveillance Report*, November, 2010, page 4.

PTSD

Overview

According to current diagnostic criteria[45] for PTSD (*see text box, below*), a person must experience a traumatic event involving death or serious injury, or a threat to the physical integrity of self or others, and react to the trauma with intense horror, fear, or helplessness. Sometime after that trauma, the person must also develop symptoms that cause clinically significant distress or impairment lasting for more than one month. Those symptoms must include symptoms from each of the following three symptom clusters:

- Reexperiencing the traumatic event, such as having recurring and distressing recollections or nightmares;
- Avoidance of stimuli associated with the trauma, such as thoughts, feelings, and conversations, along with diminished responsiveness and loss of interest in activities; and
- Hyperarousal, such as irritability, anger, hypervigilance, insomnia, or difficulty with concentration.

The formal DSM-IV-TR diagnostic criteria are below:

DSM-IV-TR Diagnostic Criteria for 309.81 Post-traumatic Stress Disorder

A. The person has been exposed to a traumatic event in which both of the following were present:

1) the person experienced, witnessed, or was confronted with an event or events that involved actual or threatened death or serious injury, or a threat to the physical integrity of self or others.
2) the person's response involved intense fear, helplessness, or horror.

B. The traumatic event is persistently reexperienced in one (or more) of the following ways:

1) recurrent and intrusive distressing recollections of the event, including images, thoughts, or perceptions.
2) recurrent distressing dreams of the event.
3) acting or feeling as if the traumatic event were recurring (includes a sense of reliving the experience, illusions, hallucinations, and dissociative flashback episodes, including those that occur on awakening or when intoxicated).
4) intense psychological distress at exposure to internal or external cues that symbolize or resemble an aspect of the traumatic event.

C. Persistent avoidance of stimuli associated with the trauma and numbing of general responsiveness (not present before the trauma), as indicated by three (or more) of the following:

1) efforts to avoid thoughts, feelings, or conversations associated with the trauma
2) efforts to avoid activities, places or people that arouse recollections of the trauma
3) inability to recall an important aspect of the trauma
4) markedly diminished interest or participation in significant activities
5) feeling of detachment or estrangement from others
6) restricted range of affect (e.g., unable to have loving feelings)
7) sense of a foreshortened future (e.g., does not expect to have a career, marriage, children, or a normal life span)

D. Persistent symptoms of increased arousal (not present before the trauma), as indicated by two (or more) of the following:

1) difficulty falling or staying asleep
2) irritability or outbursts of anger
3) difficulty concentrating
4) hyper vigilance
5) exaggerated startle response

E. Duration of the disturbance (symptoms in Criteria B,C, and D) is more than 1 month.

F. The disturbance causes clinically significant distress or impairment in social, occupational, or ther important areas of functioning.

Source: American Psychiatric Association, Diagnostic and Statistical Manual of Mental Disorders Fourth Edition Text Revision DSM-IV-TR, 2000, pp. 467-468, notes regarding children not included.

Acute PTSD occurs when the duration of symptoms is between one and three months. Patients with symptoms extending for more than three months are considered to have chronic PTSD. Delayed-onset PTSD occurs when symptoms begin at least six months after the trauma.[46] These criteria may change with the impending issuance of a DSM-V expected sometime in 2013.

Prevalence of PTSD in the Military

In 2010, 5,959 cases of PTSD were diagnosed in active duty servicemembers, a rate of approximately 8.4 new cases per 1,000 servicemembers. Overall, 2% of active duty servicemembers had ever received a PTSD diagnosis. However, the rates of PTSD diagnoses in the Army and Marine Corps were much higher than for servicemembers in the Air Force and the Navy. In 2010, the incidence rates of new diagnoses of PTSD in the active duty Army and Marine Corps were 14.3 per 1,000 and 9.7 per 1,000, respectively, compared to incidence rates of 3.7 per 1,000 for the Navy and 3.4 per 1,000 for the Air Force.[47] (See *Figure 10.*)

Acute PTSD occurs when the duration of symptoms is between one and three months. Patients with symptoms extending for more than three months are considered to have chronic PTSD. Delayed-onset PTSD occurs when symptoms begin at least six months after the trauma.[46] These criteria may change with the impending issuance of a DSM-V expected sometime in 2013.

Prevalence of PTSD in the Military

In 2010, 5,959 cases of PTSD were diagnosed in active duty servicemembers, a rate of approximately 8.4 new cases per 1,000 servicemembers. Overall, 2% of active duty servicemembers had ever received a PTSD diagnosis. However, the rates of PTSD diagnoses in the Army and Marine Corps were much higher than for servicemembers in the Air Force and the Navy. In 2010, the incidence rates of new diagnoses of PTSD in the active duty Army and Marine Corps were 14.3 per 1,000 and 9.7 per 1,000, respectively, compared to incidence rates of 3.7 per 1,000 for the Navy and 3.4 per 1,000 for the Air Force.[47] (See *Figure 10.*)

Estimates of PTSD prevalence vary depending on the methodologies used in developing them, including the means of assessment and the characteristics of the applicable population (e.g., deployment history), among other factors. Additionally, prevalence estimates based on screening tools and reported symptoms, including the pre- and post-deployment health assessments required of all deployed servicemembers, will tend to be higher than those based on the numbers of clinical diagnoses of PTSD.[48] However, rates of PTSD incidence relying solely on PTSD diagnoses will likely underestimate the true prevalence of PTSD among the Armed Forces, given the variety of barriers to mental health treatment that exist.

According to the Veterans' Administration, studies have shown that approximately 10%-18% of combat troops serving in Iraq or Afghanistan have probable PTSD after deployment.[49]

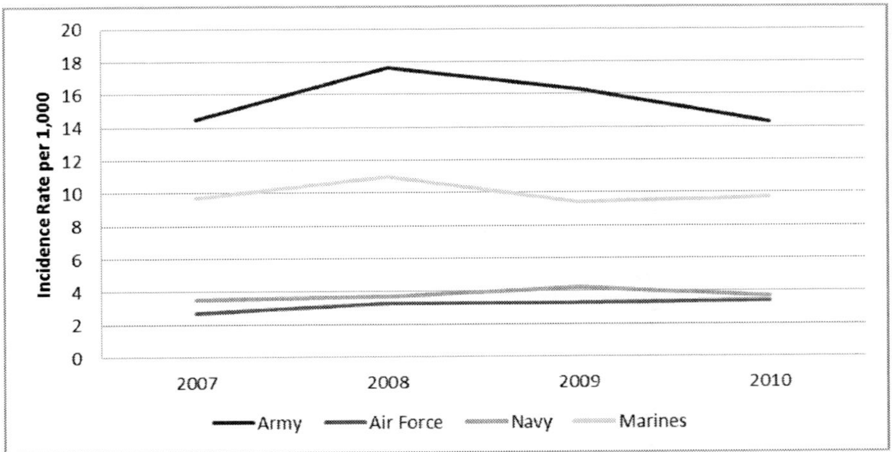

Source: Analysis by CRS. Data from "Selected Mental disorders Among Active Component Members, U.S. Armed Forces, 2007-2010." Monthly Surveillance Medical Report, Armed Forces Health Surveillance Center. Vol 17, No 11. Supplemental Report. p. 3.

Notes: Incidence rate refers to the number of new diagnoses per 1,000 person/years. Individuals are counted only once per condition. The incidence rate is distinct from the prevalence rate, or the number of individuals with a condition at any given time.

Figure 10. Incidence of PTSD by Service,Active Component. January 1, 2007-June 30, 2010.

One study, estimating PTSD prevalence based on post-deployment health assessments and reassessments (conducted 90 and 180 days after return from deployment, between 181 days and 18 months after return from deployment, and between 18 and 30 months after return from deployment), found that that probable PTSD prevalence based on reported symptoms among active duty servicemembers increased from 11.8% to 16.7% between assessments. For reservists and National Guard members, this study found that probable PTSD rates rose from 12.7% to 24.5% by the second assessment.[50] A telephone-based survey of personnel previously deployed to Iraq or Afghanistan found that approximately 14% reported symptoms indicative of probable PTSD. This study found that risk factors for PTSD included Guard or Reserve status, being of the female gender, Hispanic ethnicity, more lengthy deployments, and more extensive exposure to combat.[51] However, as discussed above, these studies relied on reported symptoms to estimate the probable prevalence of PTSD, rather than actual diagnoses of PTSD. By comparison, in the U.S. population as a whole, the proportion of those who have ever experienced PTSD was estimated at 6.8%.[52] The proportion of the U.S. population currently experiencing PTSD was estimated at 3.5%.[53]

Between January 1, 2001, and December 3, 2012, a total of 103,792 PTSD cases have been diagnosed in servicemembers who have been deployed for at least 30 days in support of OEF, OIF, or OND, according to DOD data.[54] As *Figure 11* indicates, the number of diagnoses is higher among deployed servicemembers than non-deployed servicemembers. As of July 31, 2012, approximately 2,453,036 servicemembers from the active duty, National Guard, and Reserve components have ever deployed to OEF, OIF, and/or OND.

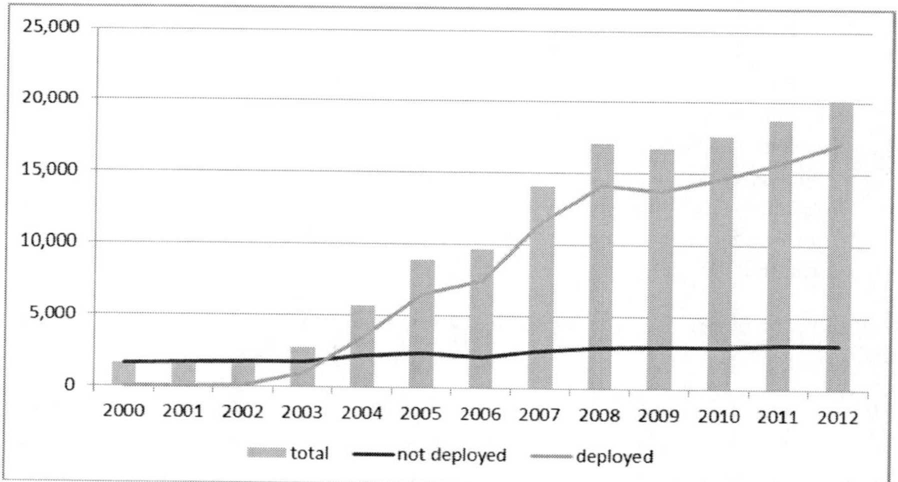

Source: Data from the Armed Forces Health Surveillance Center, Defense Medical Surveillance System and Theatre Data Store, April 2013.

Figure 11. PTSD Diagnoses Among Deployed and Non-Deployed Active Duty Servicemembers, Calendar Years 2000-2012.

Several studies have linked diagnoses of PTSD with factors common in the deployment experience. Specifically, greater combat exposure, length and/or number of deployments, perceived threat of personal danger, and deployment-related physical injuries have been associated with greater PTSD risk among servicemembers deployed to Operation Enduring Freedom, Operation Iraqi Freedom, and/or Operation New Dawn.[55] Other factors, such as perceived preparedness for combat, have also been found to mitigate the link between combat and perceived threat. Additionally, a sense of unit cohesion has been associated with a lower risk of PTSD in OEF/OIF/OND servicemembers.[56] Greater exposure of deployed Army and Marine Corps servicemembers to these aspects of combat, such as greater perceived threat of personal danger or deployment-related physical injuries, could be a factor in the higher rates of PTSD among the Army and Marine Corps, as compared to the Navy and Air Force.

Between 2001 and 2012, approximately 80% of PTSD cases among previously deployed servicemembers were diagnosed in active component servicemembers. Approximately 13% of PTSD diagnoses among previously deployed servicemembers were given to National Guard members, while 7% were given to Reserve component members. Two studies of National Guard and Reserve troops found that post-deployment stressors, including economic and relationship difficulties, also appear to be PTSD risk factors for OIF-deployed servicemembers.[57]

Alcohol and Drug-Use Disorders

Overview

The Diagnostic and Statistical Manual IV Trial Revision (DSM-IV-TR) uses specific terminology to refer to various categories of diagnoses related to alcohol and substance use. The broadest category is "substance-related disorders," which includes both "substance use disorders" (e.g., alcohol abuse or nicotine dependence) and "substance-induced disorders" (e.g., intoxication or withdrawal). Within the category of "substance use disorders," the DSM-IV-TR distinguishes between "abuse" and "dependence." (See text box below.) Substance-related disorders include dependence on and abuse of drugs, alcohol, or other substances (e.g., nicotine). A diagnosis of dependence requires at least three of seven diagnostic symptoms (e.g., tolerance or withdrawal). Substance use that does not meet criteria for dependence, but leads to clinically significant distress or impairment, is called abuse.[58] Each diagnosis is specific to the substance, so an individual may have multiple diagnoses of abuse or dependence—one for each substance (e.g., marijuana dependence and cocaine abuse).[59]

DSM-IV-TR Criteria for Substance Abuse

A maladaptive pattern of substance use, leading to clinically significant impairment or distress, as manifested by one (or more) of the following, occurring at any time in the same 12 month period:

1) recurrent substance use resulting in a failure to fulfill major role obligations at work, school or home
2) recurrent substance use in situations where it is physically hazardous
3) recurrent substance-related legal problems
4) continued substance use despite having persistent or recurrent social or interpersonal problems caused or exacerbated by the effects of the substance

DSM-IV-TR Criteria for Substance Dependence

A maladaptive pattern of substance use, leading to clinically significant impairment or distress, as manifested by three (or more) of the following, occurring at any time in the same 12-month period:

(1) tolerance, as defined by either of the following:
1) a need for markedly increased amounts of the substance to achieve intoxication or desired effect
2) markedly diminished effect with continued use of the same amount of the substance
(2) withdrawal, as manifested by either of the following:
3) the characteristic withdrawal syndrome for the substance
4) the same (or a closely related) substance is taken to relieve or avoid withdrawal symptoms
(3) the substance is often taken in larger amounts or over a longer period than was intended
(4) there is a persistent desire or unsuccessful efforts to cut down or control substance use
(5) a great deal of time is spent in activities necessary to obtain the substance (e.g., visiting multiple doctors or driving long distances), use the substance (e.g., chain-smoking), or recover from its effects
(6) important social, occupational, or recreational activities are given up or reduced because of substance use
(7) the substance use is continued despite knowledge of having a persistent or recurrent physical or psychological problem that is likely to have been caused or exacerbated by the substance (e.g., current cocain use despite recognition of cocaine-induced depression, or continued drinking despite recognition than an ulcer was made worse by alcohol consumption)

Source: American Psychiatric Association, Diagnostic and Statistical Manual of Mental Disorders Fourth Edition Text Revision DSM-IV-TR, 2000, p. 197, notes not included.

Alcohol Use Disorder Prevalence in the Military

Alcohol-related diagnoses and medical encounters in the active duty forces have increased since 2001, with the sharpest increases since 2007. (See *Figure 12*.) Between 2001 and 2010, 190,302 servicemembers had at least one medical encounter where they received an acute alcohol diagnosis, such as drunkenness, excessive blood alcohol content, or alcohol poisoning. Approximately 21% of these were considered recurrent acute cases, with at least three medical encounters with acute alcohol diagnoses.[60] However, over 90% of these recurrent acute cases likely represent treatment encounters, rather than recurrent acute cases. Approximately 4% of all coded acute alcohol diagnoses represent actual recurrent cases.[61] Over the same time period (2001–2010), over 141,000 active duty servicemembers had a medical encounter in which they received a diagnosis connected to alcohol abuse or dependence, such as alcohol abuse or alcoholic liver disease.[62]

In a 2008 survey of servicemembers, 47% self-reported as binge drinkers and 5% reported possible dependence.[63]

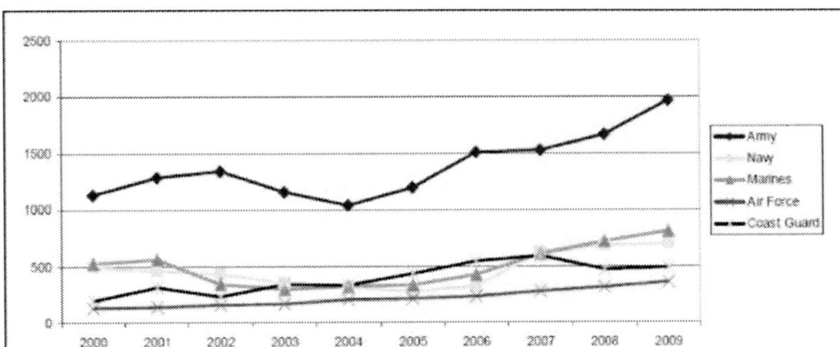

Source: Institute of Medicine, "Substance Use Disorders in the U.S. Armed Forces," 2012, p. 2-22. Citing Department of Defense, Office of the Undersecretary of Defense, "Comprehensive Plan on Prevention, Diagnosis, and Treatment of Substance Use Disorders and Disposition of Substance Use Offenders in the Armed Forces," 2011.

Notes: Incidence rates per 100,000.

Figure 12. Rates of Alcohol-Related Diagnoses Among the Active Duty Component, 2000-2009.

Drug-Use Disorder Prevalence in the Military

Between 2000 and 2011, drug abuse disorders accounted for 4% of mental disorders diagnosed among the active duty forces, with a total of 73,623 diagnoses. Though rates dipped in 2011, the rate of drug disorder diagnoses had risen between 2000 and 2009.[64] (See *Figure 13*.) The increase in substance abuse disorders is often connected to deployment. Incidence rates of cannabis and cocaine use declined, while rates of opioid and "mixed/other" substance abuse increased sharply. (See *Figure 14*.) This rise potentially reflects an increase in the misuse of prescription drugs. While overall drug use is lower in the military than civilian populations, prescription drug abuse has recently been increasing at a greater rate in the military than among the civilian population.[65] Substance abuse disorder diagnoses declined with increasing age, time in service, rank, and number of combat deployments. Rates of substance abuse diagnoses were 1.8 times greater among the youngest servicemembers than older servicemembers, while junior enlisted servicemembers had diagnoses of substance abuse disorders at a rate 17.6 times higher than officers. Substance abuse rates were consistently highest in the Army, followed by the Marine Corps.

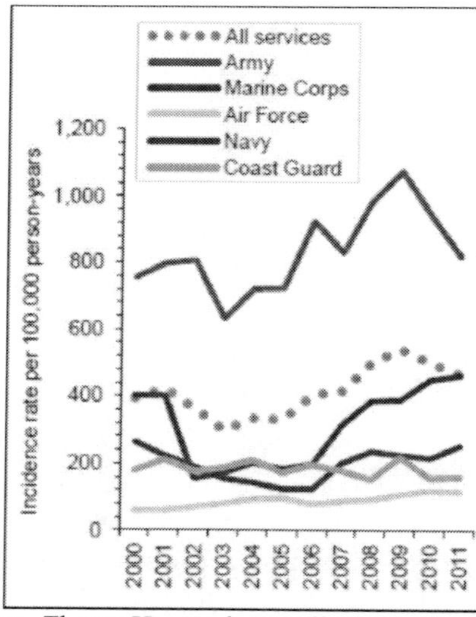

Source: Servies, Tammy, Zheng Hu, and Angelia Eick-Cost, et al., "Substance Use Disorders in the U.S. Armed Forces, 2000-2011," Medical Surveillance Monthly Report, 19(11) November 2012, p. 11.

Figure 13. Incidence Rate of Substance Abuse Disorder Diagnoses. (By service, 2000-2011)

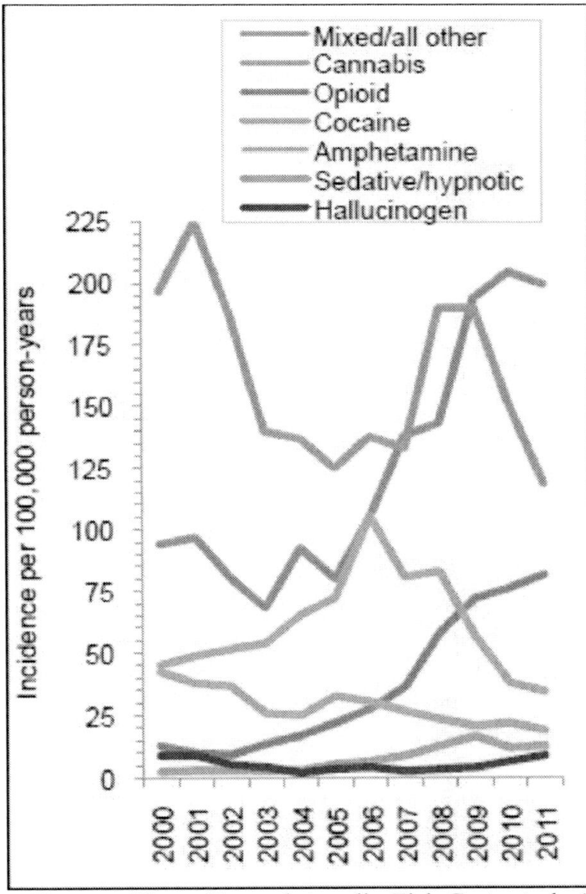

Source: Servies, Tammy, Zheng Hu, and Angelia Eick-Cost, et al., "Substance Use Disorders in the U.S. Armed Forces, 2000-2011," Medical Surveillance Monthly Report, 19(11) November 2012, p. 11.

Figure 14. Incidence Rate of Substance Abuse Disorder Diagnoses. (By drug type, 2000-2011)

A 2008 health survey of servicemembers found a decrease in illegal drug use since the 2005 survey, but an increase in prescription drug misuse, predominantly prescription pain medication. (See *Figure 15.)* Researchers have suggested that these increases in self-reported drug misuse can be partially attributed to improve survey design, as well as to increased deployments and associated diagnoses of pain disorders, PTSD, and other mental disorders.[66]

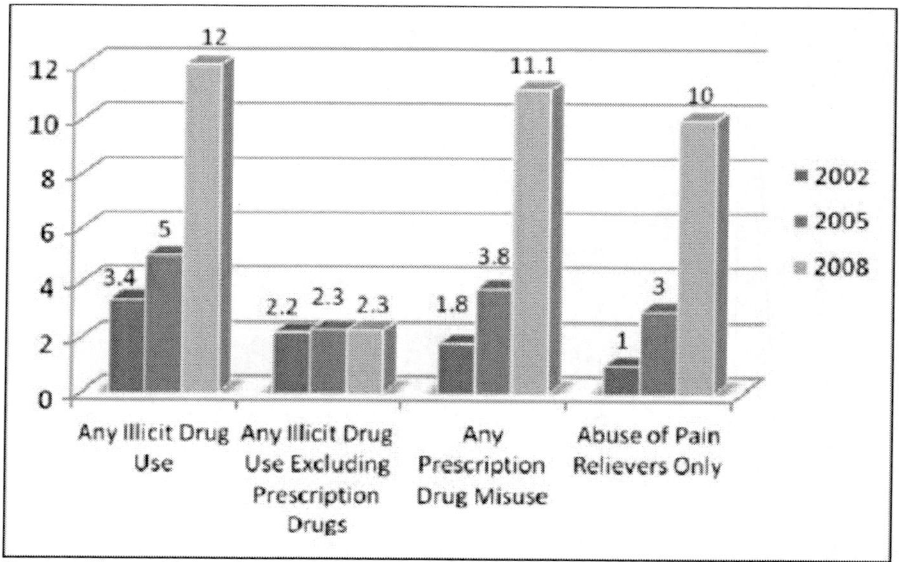

Source: Sirratt, Deborah, Alfred Ozanian, and Barbara Traenkner, "Epidemiology and Prevention of Substance Abuse Disorders in the Military," Military Medicine, 177, August Supplement 2012, p. 23.

Notes: Data from the 2002, 2005, and 2008 Health Related Behaviors Surveys. Accordingly, these figures represent self-reported rates of illicit drug use, rather than diagnosed incidences of substance abuse disorders.

Figure 15. Illicit Drug Misuse by Servicemembers, 2002-2008.

Depressive Disorders

Overview

Depression, formally diagnosed as major depressive disorder (see text box) is a mental disorder characterized by episodes of all-encompassing low mood accompanied by low self-esteem and loss of interest or pleasure in normally enjoyable activities.

Major depressive disorder is a very common mental disorder in the United States, affecting approximately 16% of adults across their lifetimes, and approximately 6.6% of adults in any 12- month period.

In a subset of the overall U.S. population with the same socio-demographic characteristics of the U.S. Army, the estimated prevalence of major depression was 1.3%.[67]

DSM-IV-TR Criteria for Major Depressive Episode

A. Five (or more) of the following symptoms have been present during the same 2-week period and represent a change from previous functioning; at least one of the symptoms is either (1) depressed mood or (2) loss of interest or pleasure.

Note: Do not include symptoms that are clearly due to a general medical condition, or mood-incongruent delusions or hallucinations.

1) depressed mood most of the day, nearly every day, as indicated by either subjective report (e.g., feels sad or empty) or observation made by others (e.g., appears tearful).
2) markedly diminished interest or pleasure in all, or almost all, activities most of the day, nearly every day (as indicated by either subjective account or observation made by others)
3) significant weight loss when not dieting or weight gain (e.g., a change of more than 5% of body weight in a month), or decrease or increase in appetite nearly every day.
4) insomnia or hypersomnia nearly every day
5) psychomotor agitation or retardation nearly every day (observable by others, not merely subjective feelings of restlessness or being slowed down)
6) fatigue or loss of energy nearly every day
7) feelings of worthlessness or excessive or inappropriate guilt (which may be delusional) nearly every day (not merely self-reproach or guilt about being sick)
8) diminished ability to think or concentrate, or indecisiveness, nearly every day (either by subjective account or as observed by others)
9) recurrent thoughts of death (not just fear of dying), recurrent suicidal ideation without a specific plan, or a suicide attempt or a specific plan for committing suicide

B The symptoms do not meet criteria for a Mixed Episode.

C The symptoms cause clinically significant distress or impairment in social, occupational, or other important areas of functioning.

D The symptoms are not due to the direct physiological effects of a substance (e.g., drug of abuse, a medication) or a general medical condition (e.g., hypothyroidism).

E The symptoms are not better accounted for by Bereavement, i.e., after the loss of a loved one, the symptoms persist for longer than 2 months or are characterized by marked functional impairment, morbid preoccupation with worthlessness, suicidal ideation, psychotic symptoms, or psychomotor retardation.

Source: American Psychiatric Association, Diagnostic and Statistical Manual of Mental Disorders Fourth Edition Text Revision DSM-IV-TR, 2000, p. 356, notes not included.

Prevalence in the Military

Among active duty troops, the prevalence of major depressive disorder for never-deployed troops was estimated at 5.7%, based on a meta-analysis of previous studies. The prevalence of major depressive disorder among currently deployed servicemembers was estimated at 12%, and at approximately 13% for previously deployed servicemembers.[68]

One limitation of this analysis was that it was not able to control for those servicemembers who did not respond to surveys or screenings, potentially underrepresenting servicemembers with high risk of mental disorders in the survey data. A second limitation is that the sampling within some of the individual studies over-represented combat units in the Armed Forces, and over-represented the months just before deployment and just after redeployment.

According to analysis by the Armed Forces Health Surveillance center using the number of diagnoses of major depressive disorder among the active duty forces, the percentage of the active duty forces ever diagnosed with major depressive disorder rose from 4.4% in 2007 to 5.1% in 2010, while the incidence rate of new diagnoses rose to 19.2 per 1,000 per year in 2009 from 17.3 per 1,000 per person per year in 2007 before declining to 15.1 per 1,000 per year in 2010.69 (See Figure 16.)

Limited data are available about the rates of major depressive disorder among the individual services. However, data on diagnoses of major depressive disorder among the services allow for limited comparison of the incidence rates between the services.

The incidence rate of diagnoses of major depressive disorder is highest among the Army over this four-year period, peaking at 28.8 per 1,000 per year in 2009.[70]

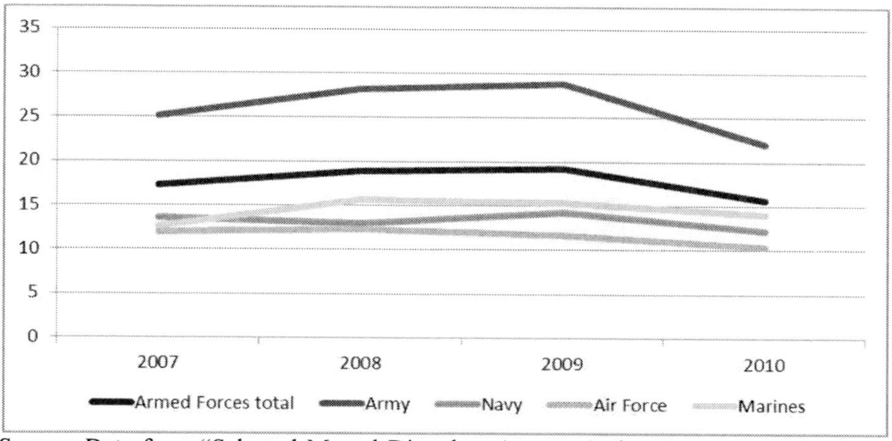

Source: Data from "Selected Mental Disorders Among Active Component Members, U.S. Armed Forces, 2007- 2010," Monthly Surveillance Medical Report, Armed Forces Health Surveillance Center. Vol. 17, No 11. Supplemental Report, p. 3.

Notes: Incidence rates include new cases per 1,000 persons per year. Individuals are counted only once per condition, in the year during which the first medical encounter for the mental health condition occurred.

Figure 16. Incidence Rates of Major Depressive Disorder Among the Active Component Services, 2007-2010.

Adjustment Disorder

Overview

Adjustment disorder is a psychological response to one or more stressors, including life events such as divorce or a period of unemployment. The diagnosis includes four components: the stressor(s), symptoms, the lack of an alternative explanation for the symptoms, and the timing of the symptoms. Stressors may occur once, multiple times, or be chronic.

A diagnosis of adjustment disorder does not require specific symptoms. Rather, it requires clinically significant distress, such as anxiety or depressed mood, or impairment in functioning, such as social or occupational problems. A diagnosis of adjustment disorder is a residual category for cases that do not meet the criteria for another mental disorder. Finally, a diagnosis of adjustment disorder must take the timing of the symptoms relative to the stressor(s) into account. In order for a diagnosis of adjustment disorder to be appropriate, symptoms must appear within three months of the onset of the stressor(s) and resolve within six months of the termination of the stressor(s).[71]

Adjustment disorder is acute if symptoms resolve within six months in total, and chronic if symptoms persist for longer than six months.

Prevalence in the Military

Between 2000 and 2011, adjustment disorders accounted for 26% of mental disorders diagnosed among the active duty forces, for a total of 471,833 diagnoses. The rates of adjustment disorder diagnoses increased by 98% between 2000 and 2011.[72]

Other Conditions

Overview

The Diagnostic and Statistical Manual also provides a means of recording other circumstances of concern that are clinically significant, but that are not diagnosable mental disorders. These are called "V codes" (not to be confused with the DSM-V issued by the APA in May 2013, the successor edition to the DSM-IV-TR) and identify conditions other than a disease or injury. These codes are also used to report significant factors that may influence present or future care or may be a focus of clinical attention. V codes are not necessarily a primary diagnosis.

V codes in the DSM-IV-TR include codes for problems in partner relationships; other family relationships; maltreatment, such as physical abuse or sexual abuse; and life circumstances, including bereavement and occupational, religious, academic, identity, or acculturation problems. For details on the use of V codes for mental health issues in the military, please see *Appendix A.*

Prevalence in the Military

Active duty servicemembers have been provided assistance for other mental issues, such as difficulties related to life circumstances (including pending, current, or recent deployments), difficulty in a partner relationship, or mental, behavioral, or substance use difficulties. Between 2000 and 2011, over 425,000 active duty servicemembers sought help for these mental health problems. This number does not include servicemembers who received diagnoses for specific mental disorders.

Overall, incidence rates of DSM "V codes" related to mental health issues have declined overall from 2000 through 2011 by approximately 30%, but with a sharp increase between 2004 and 2005. Incidence rates and numbers of DSM "V codes" connected to mental, behavioral, and substance abuse issues are the only category of mental health problems to have increased between 2000 and 2011, increasing by approximately 120%. (See *Figure 17.)*

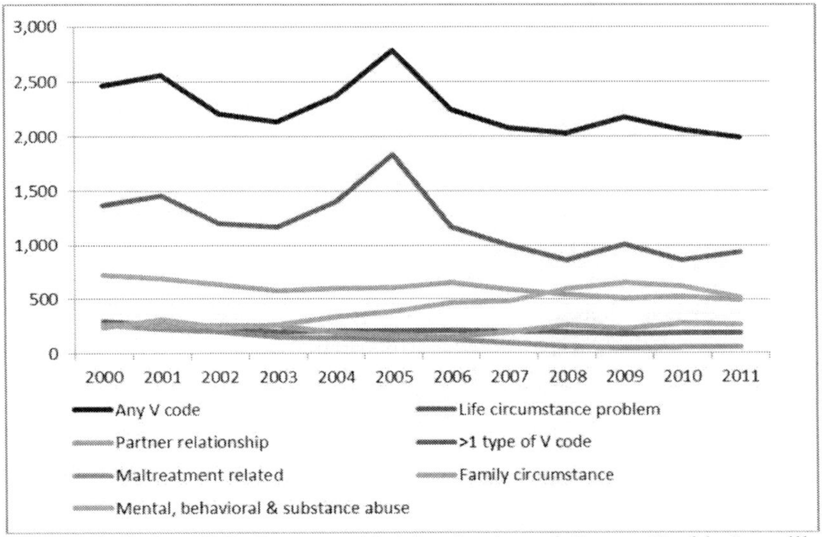

Source: Analysis by CRS. Data provided by the Armed Forces Health Surveillance Center, expanded from the data presented in "Mental Disorders And Mental Health Problems, Active Component, U.S. Armed Forces, 2000-2011," Medical Surveillance Monthly Report, 19(6), June 2012.

Notes: The number of active duty members who sought treatment for other mental health problems between 2000 and 2011 totaled approximately 425,000. These numbers do not include servicemembers who received a diagnosis for a specific mental disorder.

Incidence rate is number of diagnoses per 100,000 person-years, for example, for an incidence rate of 7,000 out of a population of 100,000 observed for one year, 7,000 new diagnoses would be expected. For a population of 50,000 observed for one year (50,000 person years), or a population of 100,000 observed for six months (also 50,000 person-years), 3,500 new diagnoses would be expected.

Figure 17. Incidence of Other Mental Health Problems. (Active Duty Forces, 2000-2011).

While these other mental health issues are not themselves mental health diagnoses, they play an important role in the psychological health of the active duty force. For example, one study of servicemembers who have received mental health care for "V code" conditions related to family or partner problems found they were at increased risk of death by suicide.[73]

Traumatic Brain Injury (TBI)

Overview

The Centers for Disease Control and Prevention defines TBI as an injury to the head arising from blunt or penetrating trauma, or from acceleration-deceleration forces that result in one or more of the following:

- decreased level of consciousness;
- amnesia regarding the event itself or events preceding or following the injury;
- skull fracture;
- a neurological or neuropsychological abnormality such as disorientation, agitation, or confusion; or
- an intracranial lesion such as a traumatic intracranial hematoma, cerebral contusion, or penetrating injury.[74]

Neurologists classify the severity of the TBI as mild, moderate, severe, or penetrating. (See *Table 5.*) Penetrating TBIs are open head injuries in which the dura mater, the outer layer of the meninges (the membranes that surround the brain), is penetrated. Because TBI has a readily observable physical cause, it is much different than psychological health conditions. Nevertheless, as discussed below, there may be associations between TBI and other mental health diagnoses.

Table 5. Symptoms and Severity of Non-Penetrating Traumatic Brain Injuries

Confusion or Disorientation		Loss of Consciousness	Memory Loss	MRI or CT results
Mild (Concussion)	< 24 hrs	< 30 minutes	< 24 hrs	normal
Moderate	> 24 hrs	> 30 minutes < 24 hrs	> 24 hrs, < 7 days	normal or abnormal
Severe	> 24 hrs	> 24 hrs	> 7 days	normal or abnormal

Source: Defense and Veterans' Brain Injury Center (DVBIC), "DOD Numbers for Traumatic Brain Injury Worldwide—Totals," http://www.dvbic.org/sites/default/files/uploads/dod-tbi-2000-2012.pdf, accessed 7/26/2013.

TBI is a common injury from the wars in Iraq and Afghanistan,[75] and is a signature injury of improvised explosive device (IED) blasts. However, according to the Defense and Veteran's Brain Injury Center, 84% of TBIs occur in a non-deployed setting. Common causes of TBI include crashes in privately owned and military vehicles, falls, sports and recreation activities, and military training.[76]

Symptoms of mild TBI often include headache; dizziness; weakness; sensitivity to light or sound; cognitive symptoms, including difficulty with attention, memory, or language; and psychological symptoms, including irritability, depression, anxiety, or personality changes.[77] Symptoms of mild TBI often overlap with symptoms of other psychological issues, and therefore require concurrent treatment. Approximately 85%-90% of servicemembers who have sustained a combat-related, mild TBI recover with no lasting clinical difficulties.[78]

Symptoms of moderate or severe TBI often include longer periods of confusion or disorientation, loss of consciousness, and memory loss. MRI or CT results may be normal or abnormal. Moderate or severe TBI sustained in combat requires early recognition of the injury and speedy evacuation to a combat support hospital or trauma center where specialized neurological care is available. Effective treatment and decisions during the period immediately after brain injury are essential for optimal outcomes.[79]

Prevalence in the Military

Since 2001, servicemembers have experienced about 255,852 TBIs, including approximately 212,741 incidences of mild TBI, approximately 20,168 incidences of moderate TBI, approximately 6,472 incidences of severe TBI/penetrating head injuries, and 16,471 unclassifiable TBIs. (See *Figure 18.*)

Incidents of mild TBI rose sharply between 2005 and 2007, due in part to more aggressive screening measures for mild TBI instituted in 2006.[80] (See *Figure 19.*) Since March 2006, all servicemembers returning from theatre and all servicemembers arriving at Landsruhe Medical Center receive a TBI screen regardless of other medical conditions. Diagnoses of TBI in deployed settings nearly doubled between 2010 and 2011, due in part to a greater focus on identifying and treating TBIs among deployed servicemembers,[81] as reflected in the July 2010 "Policy Guidance for the Management of Concussion/Mild Traumatic Brain Injury in the Deployed Setting."[82] These policies require TBI screening for those exposed to potentially concussive events, and medical evaluation for all servicemembers who sustained physical injury, exhibited

TBI symptoms such as headache or ear ringing, or were within 50 meters of a blast.[83]

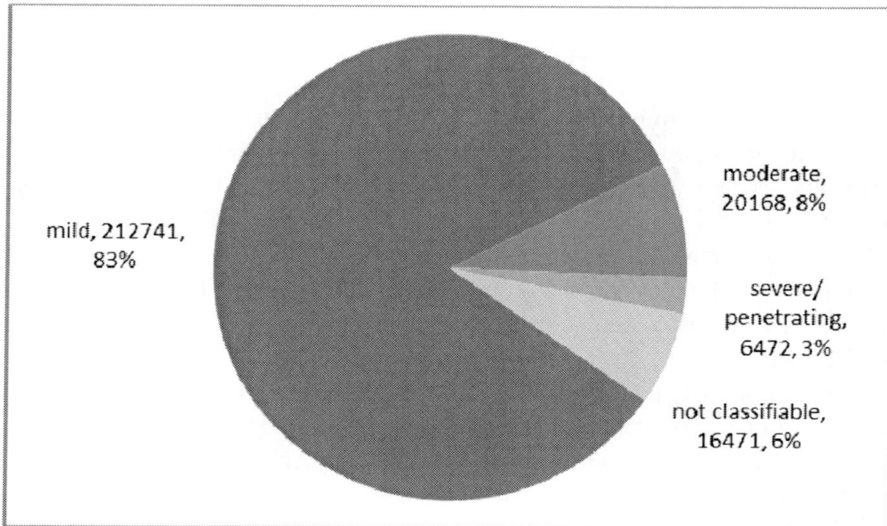

Source: Data from the Armed Forces Medical Surveillance Center, Defense Medical Surveillance System (DMSS), and the Theater Medical Data Store (TMDS), April 2013.

Notes: The diagnosis and severity of injury were determined using ICD-9 codes. Each data set is based on garrison medical encounters in the Defense Medical Surveillance System, Standard Ambulatory Data Records, Health Care Service Record and TRICARE Encounter Data feeds, and theater medical encounters in the Theater Medical Data Store. Servicemembers may be counted only once, at the most severe level of injury. Therefore, these data cannot track multiple TBIs experienced by the same servicemember.

These data include TBIs for active duty and activated Guard and Reserve members.

Figure 18. TBI Injuries by Severity, 2001-2012.

Screening for TBI is indicated if the servicemember has been exposed to any mechanism of injury that could potentially cause TBI, for example, blast exposures, falls, or vehicle crashes.[84] According to researchers, reliance on servicemember self-reports and co-occurring conditions can make TBI screening challenging. The deployed acute screening tool for concussion, the Concussion Management Algorithm, was updated in early 2012.[85] Screening for concussion is required for any servicemember who is in a vehicle with a blast event, collision, or rollover; is within 50 meters of a blast; sustains a direct blow to the head; or at the direction of their commander, for example, with repeated exposures to injury mechanisms. All exposed servicemembers, including those who test negative for concussion, are mandated to rest for 24 hours before returning to duty.[86]

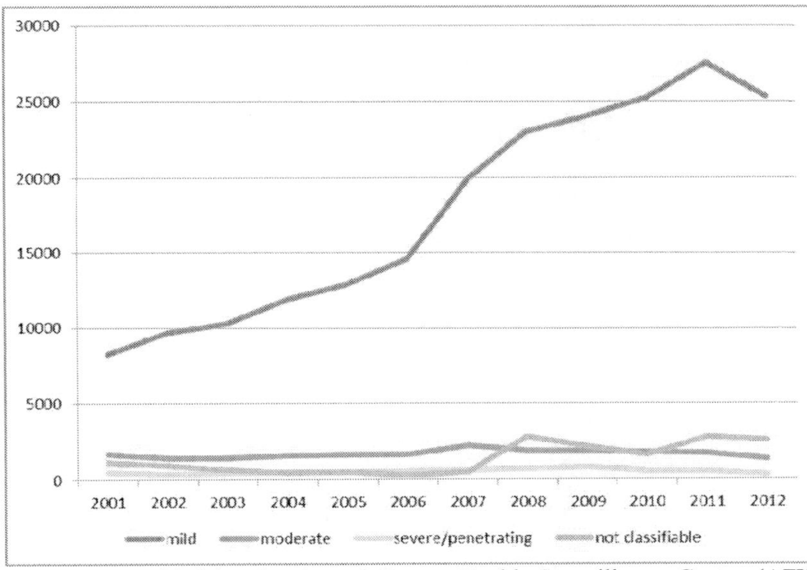

Source: Data provided by the Armed Forces Health Surveillance Center (AFHSC) April 2013.

Notes: The diagnosis and severity of injury were determined using ICD-9 codes. Each data set is based on garrison medical encounters in the Defense Medical Surveillance System, Standard Ambulatory Data Records, Health Care Service Record and TRICARE Encounter Data feeds, and theater medical encounters in the Theater Medical Data Store. Servicemembers may be counted only once, at the most severe level of injury. Therefore, these data cannot track multiple TBIs experienced by the same servicemember.

These data include TBIs for active duty and activated Guard and Reserve members.

Figure 19. TBI Incidence by Severity, 2001-2012.

Causes

All services have experienced a rise in the number of TBIs, although the rate of increase has been much greater for the Army and Marines Corps than for the Navy and Air Force. When broken out by type of TBI (mild, moderate, severe/penetrating, or unclassifiable), Army servicemembers have experienced the greatest number of TBIs of each type. (See *Figure 20.*)

Over the 12 years between 2000 and 2011, approximately 175,290 active component servicemembers had at least one TBI diagnosis. Records of the cause of injury were not available for over 60% of these diagnoses. Between 2008 and 2011, for the 24,115 servicemembers where the cause of the TBI was recorded, approximately 74% were the result of accidents, including motor vehicle accidents (20%), falls (20%), or striking or being struck by an object (15%). Assaults and battle injuries were each the reported cause of 11% of TBIs where the cause was recorded. In combat theatres, 6,950 TBIs were diagnosed between 2008 and 2011. While only 15% of these diagnoses had cause-of-injury codes, nearly all of these TBIs were attributed to combat injuries (88%) or gun/explosive accidents (7%).[87]

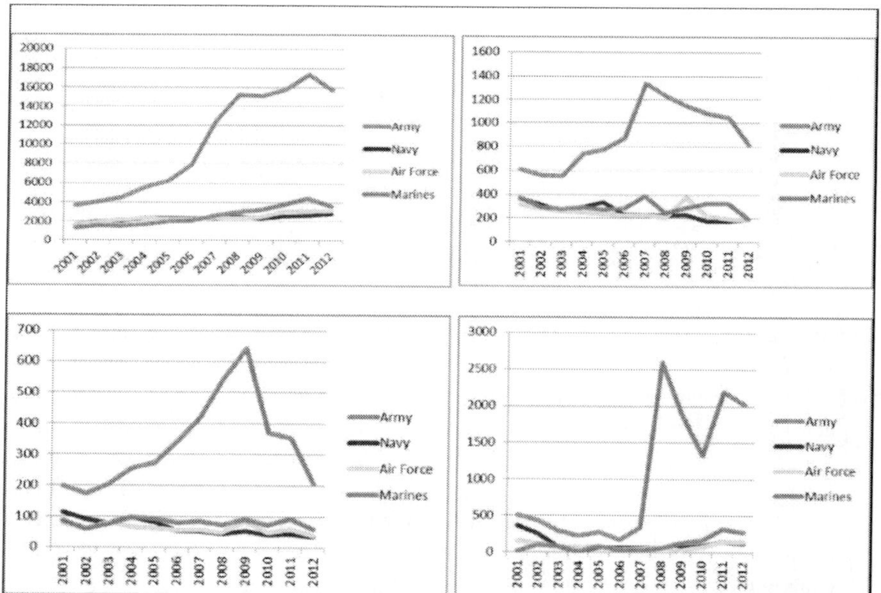

Source: Data provided by the Armed Forces Health Surveillance Center (AFHSC).

Notes: The diagnosis and severity of injury were determined using ICD-9 codes. Each data set is based on garrison medical encounters in the Defense Medical Surveillance System, Standard Ambulatory Data Records, Health Care Service Record and TRICARE Encounter Data feeds, and theater medical encounters in the Theater Medical Data Store. Servicemembers may be counted only once, at the most severe level of injury. Therefore, these data cannot track multiple TBIs experienced by the same servicemember. These data include TBIs for active duty and activated Guard and Reserve members.

Figure 20. TBIs by Severity and Service, 2001-2011.

Associated Illnesses

A 2008 Institute of Medicine report conducted a meta-analysis and review of research on the long-term consequences of TBI. Studies have found TBI and brain injury survivors are at elevated risk for depression, generalized anxiety disorder, and PTSD.[88] One study of TBI and associated psychiatric illnesses found that 49% of those with moderate or severe TBI had evidence of psychiatric illness, compared to 34% in the mild TBI group and 18% of those without TBI.

The risk generally scales with the increased severity of a TBI.[89] There is also limited evidence that suggests an association between TBI and completed suicide, although there is insufficient evidence to determine whether there is an association between TBI and attempted suicide.[90] Among Gulf War veterans, there is limited/suggestive evidence of an association between mild TBI and PTSD.[91]

The 2008 Institute of Medicine report also concluded that TBI is associated with aggression, irritability, emotional reactivity, sleep disorders, drug and alcohol abuse and dependence, and personality disorders, among other personality and behavioral outcomes related to poor psychosocial functioning.[92]

Several studies have shown a connection between TBI and a greater risk of developing dementia. A 2010 study of 280,000 veterans at the San Francisco VA Medical Center found that 15% of veterans diagnosed with TBI developed dementia, compared to 7% of those without a diagnosis.[93] The 2008 Institute of Medicine meta-analysis and review of research on the long-term consequences of TBI concluded that that there is evidence of an association between moderate or severe TBI and dementia of the Alzheimer type and Parkinson's disease. It also found that there is limited or suggestive evidence between mild TBI and some types of dementia.[94]

Suicide

Overview

Beginning in 2010, suicide has been the second-leading cause of death for active duty servicemembers, behind only war injuries.[95] Researchers have suggested that, similar to suicides among civilians, suicides by servicemembers are often impulsive acts triggered by various stressors, including relationship problems, financial or legal problems, or financial problems.[96]

Prevalence in the Military

Suicides among the active duty forces have increased between 1998 and 2012, rising from approximately 200 deaths by suicide in 1998 to 349 in 2012. (See *Figure 21.*)

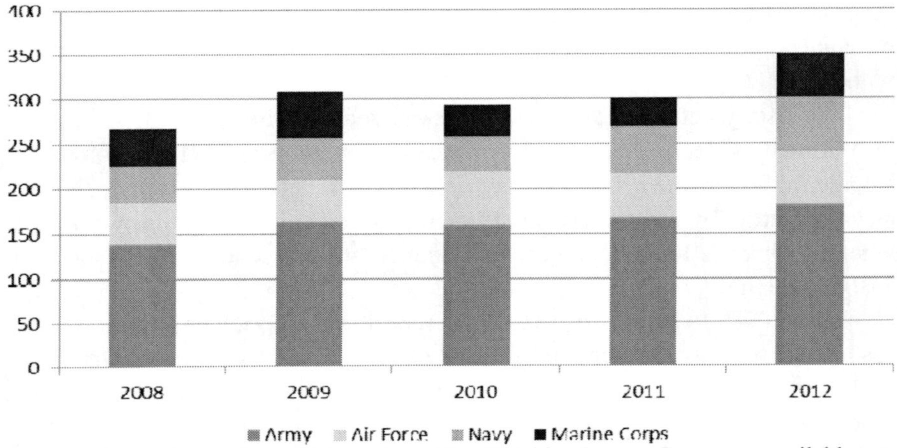

Source: Data from the 2008-2011 DOD Suicide Event Reports, available at https://dodser.t2.health.mil/ welcome, 2012 Data from the Armed Forces Health Surveillance Center, March 2013.

Notes: These figures include some probable suicides that have not been definitively determined to be suicides by April 1 each year, when data for each report are compiled.

Figure 21. Suicides Among the Active Duty Forces, by Service. (2008-2012)

Between 1998 and 2011, 2,990 servicemembers on active duty have died by suicide, with an incidence rate of approximately 14 per 100,000 person years. However, the suicide rate among active duty servicemembers has sharply increased since 2005, reaching a peak of 18.5 per 100,000 in 2009 and declining slightly to 17.5 per 100,000 in 2010 and 18 per 100,000 in 2011.[97] (See *Figure 22.*) While the rates of suicide in the Armed Forces overall have increased between 1998 and 2011, the rates remain lower than for comparable civilian populations. Lower suicide rates among the Armed Forces have been attributed to a variety of factors, including the servicemember's full-time employment; "healthy-worker" effects, including a sense of belonging and purpose among active duty servicemembers; and universal access to health care among the military population.[98]

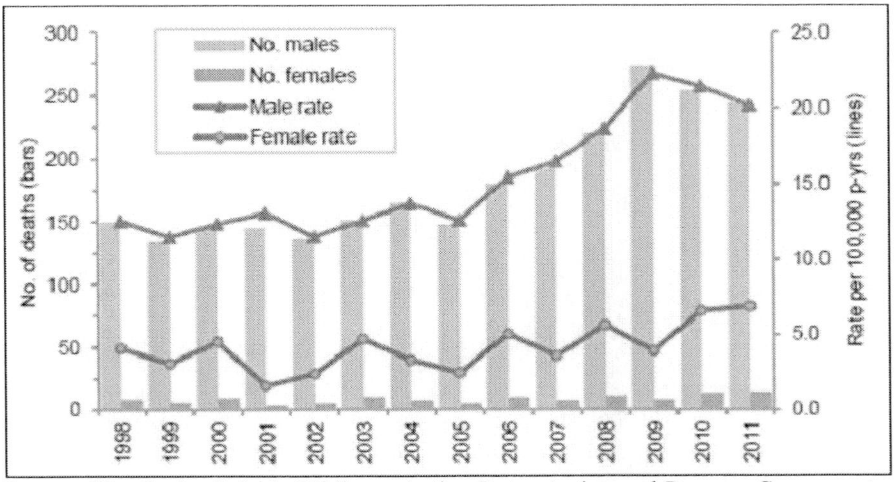

Source: "Deaths by Suicide While on Active Duty, Active and Reserve Components, U.S. Armed Forces, 1998- 2011," Medical Surveillance Monthly Report, vol. 19, no. 6 (June 2012), p. 8.

Figure 22. Suicide in the Active Duty Forces, 1998-2011.

From 1990 to 2000, before the wars in Iraq and Afghanistan, the incidence of suicide in active duty forces was approximately 25% lower than in comparable civilian populations, approximately 8.31 per 100,000 people per year among the active duty forces, as compared to 12.31 per person per year in the civilian population.[99] Between 1998 and 2011, researchers have estimated that if the active duty Armed Forces had the same rates of death by suicide as a comparable civilian population, the number of deaths by suicide among male active duty servicemembers would have been approximately 23% higher, resulting in an additional 598 deaths by suicide among male servicemembers.[100]

Rates of death by suicide also differ across the services. Between 1998 and 2011, the Army has experienced the greatest number of servicemember deaths by suicide, 1,370, or 46% of all servicemember deaths by suicide. (See Figure 23.) Most of the increase in suicide rates between 2000 and 2011 has been concentrated in the Army and Marine Corps. Between 2005 and 2009 the incidence of suicide has nearly doubled for Army and Marine personnel, while remaining approximately level for Navy and Air Force personnel.[101] In 2011, the suicide rate for Army personnel was approximately 23 per 100,000, while the rates for the Navy and Marine Corps were approximately 15 per 100,000 and the rate for the Air Force was approximately 13 per 100,000.

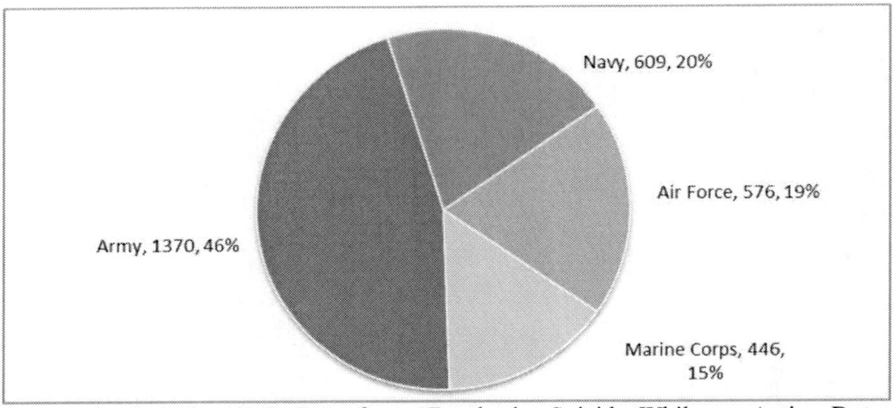

Source: Analysis by CRS. Data from "Deaths by Suicide While on Active Duty, Active and Reserve Components, U.S. Armed Forces, 1998-2011," Medical Surveillance Monthly Report, vol. 19, no. 6 (June 2012), p. 9.

Figure 23. Suicides by Service, 1998-2011.

According to the 2011 DOD Suicide Event Report, servicemembers who died by suicide in 2011 were more likely than the rest of the general military population to be male, junior enlisted (E1- E4) or high school educated, under the age of 25, and non-Hispanic white. These trends among attempted suicides and death by suicide among the active duty forces for 2011 were similar to those in 2010 and 2009, the two other calendar years for which detailed information is available.

Additionally, the suicide rate for divorced servicemembers was 55% greater than the suicide rate for married servicemembers in 2011.[102]

In general, these data regarding deaths by suicide among the active duty forces must be regarded with caution. The deaths by suicide, as captured by the Armed Forces Medical Examiner system, include only suicides that occurred during active duty military service. Therefore, these suicide figures for the active duty forces do not include deaths by suicide or suicide attempts by inactivated National Guard and Reserve members, or individuals who die by suicide after their military service has ended. In addition, suicides by various methods may be difficult to authoritatively ascertain as suicides. For example, suicides by drug overdoses or automobile accidents may be misclassified as accidents, leading to the undercounting of both deaths by suicide and suicide attempts.

Suicide and Suicide Attempt Methods

Between 1998 and 2011, firearms were the most frequently used method of suicide by active duty servicemembers, accounting for 62% of suicides among males and 42% among females. The proportion of suicides due to firearms was highest in the Reserve component, at 70%. Firearms were the most commonly used method of suicide among males of all age groups and females age 20 and over. Nearly 60% of all active duty deaths by suicide in 2011 used firearms. Non-military issue firearms were used in 49% of deaths by suicide in 2011. Hanging was the second most common cause of death by suicide, accounting for 20% of all deaths by suicide.[103]

In 2011, drug overdoses were the most common method of suicide attempts, accounting for nearly 60% of non-fatal attempted suicides. Of all suicide attempts that involved drug use, 64% involved the use of prescription drugs. 41% of all deaths by suicide or attempts at suicide involved prescription drug use. Alcohol use was involved in 31% of suicide attempts. Firearms were used in 4% of suicide attempts.[104]

Between 1998 and 2011, nearly half of active duty deaths by suicide involved personal weapons, while about 6% of suicide attempts involved firearms. (See *Figure 24.*) Firearms were present in the homes of 50% of servicemembers who died by suicide, as compared to 11% of servicemembers who attempted suicide. DOD officials are developing a suicide prevention campaign that will encourage friends and families of potentially suicidal servicemembers to safely store or voluntarily remove personal firearms from their homes.[105]

Contextual Factors

Most servicemembers who attempted suicide (76%) or died by suicide (74%) were not known to have communicated their potential for self-harm. Those who did most often communicated with spouses, friends, and other family members.[106]

Of the 301 servicemembers who died by suicide in 2011:

- 55% had no known behavioral health disorder;
- 20% had mood disorders. 11% had depression, the most common diagnosed mood disorder;
- 16% had an anxiety disorder. The most common anxiety disorder, at 6% of deaths by suicide, was PTSD;

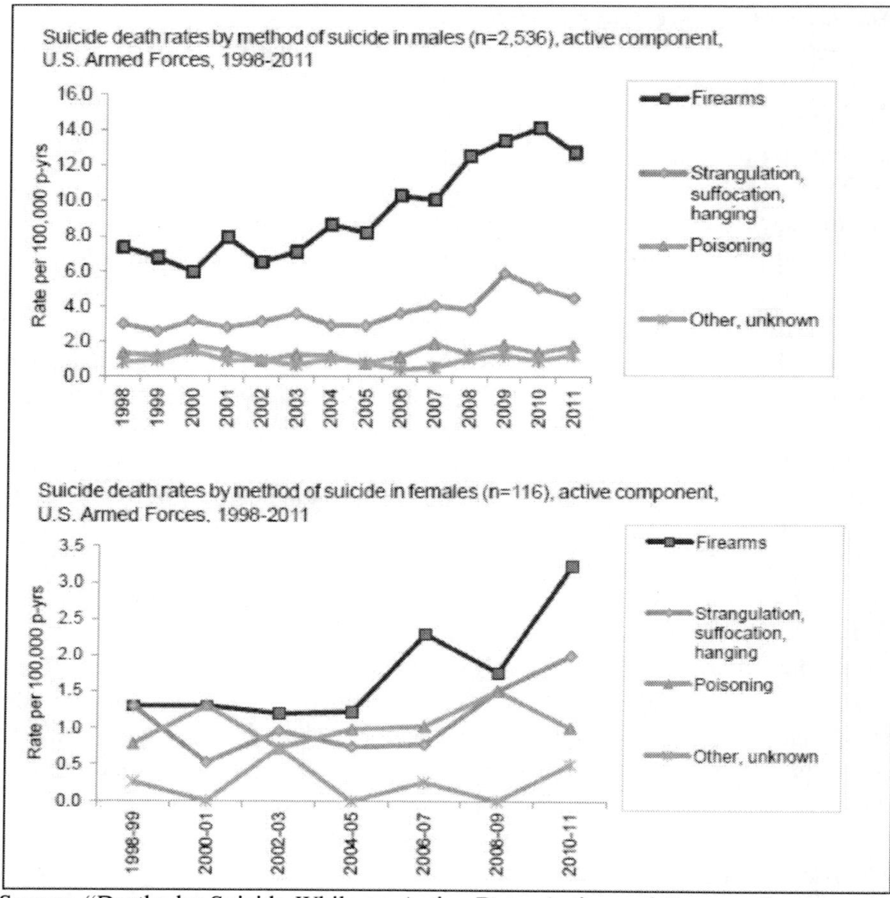

Source: "Deaths by Suicide While on Active Duty, Active and Reserve Components, U.S. Armed Forces, 1998- 2011," Medical Surveillance Monthly Report, vol. 19, no. 6 (June 2012), p. 9.

Figure 24. Suicide Rates by Method of Suicide. 1998-2011, Males and Females.

- 25% had a known history of substance abuse, while 16% received substance abuse treatment services;
- 40% received outpatient behavioral health care, while 17% had received outpatient behavioral health services within the month prior to suicide;
- 15% had received inpatient behavioral health treatment;
- 26% had a known history of psychotropic medication use, most frequently antidepressants (22%);

- 47% had experienced a failure of a spousal or intimate relationship, 27.5% within the 30 days prior to suicide;
- 18% had experienced Article 15 proceedings/non-judicial punishment, while 13% had experienced civil legal problems;
- 21% had a known history of job loss or instability, e.g., demotions; and,
- 47% had been deployed, while 8% had been deployed multiple times. 15% had direct combat experience.

In 2011, 915 active duty servicemembers attempted, but did not complete, suicide. 896 servicemembers attempted suicide once, 18 attempted suicide twice, and 1 servicemember attempted suicide three times.[107] Of the 915 active duty servicemembers who attempted suicide in 2011:

- 64% had a known history of a behavioral health disorder;
- 34% had a mood disorder, most frequently major depression (21%);
- 25% had diagnoses of anxiety disorders, most frequently PTSD (12%);
- 27% had a known history of substance abuse;
- 43% had a known history of psychotropic medication use, most frequently antidepressants (36.5%);
- 61% had received outpatient behavioral health services within the month prior to suicide;
- 52% had experienced a failure of a spousal or intimate relationship, 33% within the month prior to suicide;
- 19% had experienced Article 15 proceedings/non-judicial punishment, while 7% had experienced civil legal problems;
- 31% had a known history of job loss or instability, e.g., demotions; and
- 40% had been deployed, 4% had been deployed multiple times, and 17% had direct combat experience.

Deployments, Combat Exposure, and Psychological Health Disorders

The reasons for the higher rates in mental health diagnoses and suicide rates among Army and Marine personnel are not clear. While repeated ground combat tours would be a possible answer, according to U.S. military medical researchers, "to date no study has definitively confirmed an independent variation" of ground combat tours with servicemember suicides.[108] Researchers suggest that "the cumulative strain from the protracted war effort, across both deployed and garrison environments" may be "causing higher population prevalence of mental disorders," leading to higher suicide rates.[109]

Many Members of Congress, military leaders, and health providers have expressed concern that increased numbers of deployments and shorter "dwell" times between deployments have increased the stress and mental health toll on U.S. servicemembers. However, studies of deployed servicemembers have reached varying conclusions regarding the links between deployment(s) and various psychological health concerns, including PTSD, depression, anxiety, and stress.

Repeated Deployments

While several studies have found higher rates of mental health problems among repeat deployers than among first-time deployers, other studies have found little evidence of a causal link between repeated deployments and various mental health problems.

One possible explanation is that servicemembers who are more negatively affected by deployments are less likely to deploy again, and may leave the Armed Forces. Therefore, the servicemembers who deploy repeatedly may be more resilient.

Additionally, servicemembers with repeated deployments may gain additional knowledge, skills, and confidence in combat environments, also increasing their psychological resilience.[110]

According to an analysis of diagnoses received by previously deployed active component servicemembers, rates of diagnoses of anxiety disorders and adjustment reactions (including PTSD) rose after the first, second, and third deployments, before falling sharply for the fourth and fifth deployments.[111] A follow-up study, focusing specifically on mental health diagnoses received in the year after a servicemember returns from combat, found that among male servicemembers, diagnoses of PTSD, adjustment reactions, anxiety-related disorders, and depressive disorders were more common after second, third, and fourth deployments than first deployments. Among male servicemembers, a greater proportion was diagnosed with alcohol or drug disorders, suicidal ideation/self-inflicted injuries, and psychosocial problems after the first deployment than all following deployments.[112]

The results among female servicemembers were somewhat different. Like among male servicemembers, PTSD diagnoses increased following the second, third, and fourth deployments. However, the percentage of female servicemembers diagnosed with other mental disorders, including depressive disorders, alcohol/drug disorders, suicidal ideation/self-inflicted injury, adjustment reactions, anxiety disorders, and psychosocial problems all declined after repeated deployments.[113] (See *Figure 25*.)

Overall, for all deployed active component servicemembers, larger percentages received diagnoses of PTSD and anxiety-related disorders after the second and/or third deployment than after the first deployment. The rates of PTSD diagnoses fall sharply after the fourth and fifth deployments.[114] However, for other mental disorders than anxiety disorders and PTSD, a greater proportion of deployed servicemembers receive diagnoses after their first deployment than subsequent deployments.

Dwell Time

Quickened deployment cycles and the shorter "dwell" time between deployments are often cited as a risk factor leading to greater stress and higher rates of mental disorders among deployed servicemembers.

However, a recent analysis by the Armed Forces Health Surveillance Center found that the percentages of deployed servicemembers diagnosed with a mental disorder were greater among servicemembers with longer dwell times between deployments.

However, the study cautions that personal circumstances can greatly influence the nature, magnitude, duration, and effects of stresses related to transition and readjustment periods, such as preparing for or following a deployment.

The Armed Forces Health Surveillance Center study also speculates that the double transition from "warrior" to being fully adjusted as non-deployed back to "warrior" status may play a role. They also note that servicemembers with medical conditions associated with recent deployments may have very long dwell times and be at a higher risk of recurrent or related conditions following their deployment.[115]

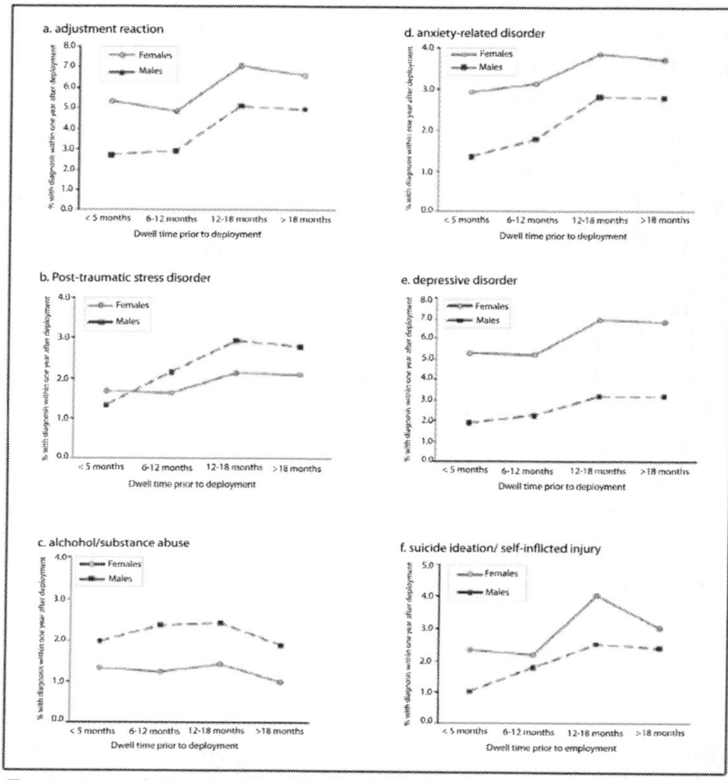

Source: From Armed Forces Health Surveillance Center, "Associations Between Repeated Deployments to Iraq (OIF/OND) and Afghanistan (OEF) and Post-deployment Illnesses and Injuries, Active Component, U.S. Armed Forces, 2003-2010," Monthly Medical Surveillance Report, 18(9), September 2011, p. 8.

Notes: These figures include deployed active component servicemembers diagnosed at non-deployed medical treatment facilities within one year of OEF/OIF/OND deployment.

Figure 25. Percentage of Deployed Servicemembers Diagnosed with Selected Mental Disorders, by "Dwell Times," by Gender, 2003-2010.

Combat-Specific and Health Care Occupations

Deployed servicemembers in health care occupations consistently had the highest rates of PTSD diagnoses, as well as diagnoses of other anxiety disorders, adjustment reactions, and depressive disorder than servicemembers in other occupations, including combat-specific occupations.

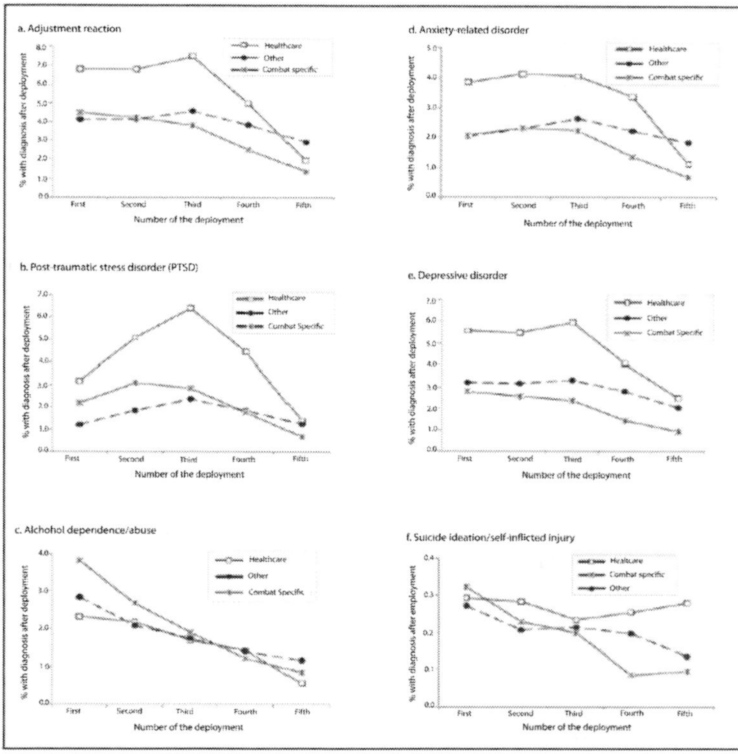

Source: From Armed Forces Health Surveillance Center, "Associations Between Repeated Deployments to Iraq (OIF/OND) and Afghanistan (OEF) and Post-Deployment Illnesses and Injuries, Active Component, U.S. Armed Forces, 2003-2010. Part II: Mental Disorders, by Gender, Age Group, Military Occupation and 'Dwell Times' Prior to Repeat (Second through Fifth) Deployments" Monthly Medical Surveillance Report, 18(9), September 2011, p. 8.

Notes: These figures include deployed active component servicemembers diagnosed at non-deployed medical treatment facilities within one year of OEF/OIF/OND deployment.

Figure 26. Percentage of Deployed Servicemembers Diagnosed with Selected Mental Disorders, by Number of Deployments and Military Occupational Group, 2003-2010.

(See Figure 26.) One possible explanation is that the consistent exposure of servicemembers in health care occupations to traumatic injuries suffered by others leads to higher rates of PTSD, as compared to the more intermittent, but more intense and personal exposures to life-threatening experiences among combat-specific occupations.

Additionally, servicemembers in health care occupations likely have a higher utilization of health care, including mental health care, than servicemembers in combat-specific occupations.[116]

Appendix A. Diagnostic Codes

Diagnostic category	ICD-9 codes
ICD-9 mental disorders	
Adjustment disorders	309.0x-309.9x (excluding 309.81)
Alcohol abuse/dependence disorders	303.xx, 305.0x
Substance abuse/dependence disorders	304.xx, 305.2x-305.9x
Anxiety disorders	300.00-300.09, 300.20-300.29,300.3
Post-traumatic stress disorder	309.81
Depressive disorders	296.20-296.35, 296.50-296.55, 296.9x, 300.4, 311
Personality disorders	301.0, 301.10, 301.11, 301.12, 301.13, 301.20, 301.21, 301.22, 301.3, 301.4, 301.50, 301.51, 301.59, 301.6, 301.7, 301.81, 301.82, 301.83, 301.84, 301.89, 301.9
Schizophrenia	295.xx
Other psychoses	293.81, 293.82, 297.0x-297.3x, 297.8, 297.9, 298.0, 298.1, 298.2, 298.3, 298.4, 298.8, 298.9
Other mental health disorder	Any other code between 290-319 (excluding 305.1, 299.xx, 315.xx, 317.xx-319.xx)
V-coded behavioral health disorder	
Partner relationship problems	V61.0x, V61.1, V61.10 (excluding V61.11, V61.12)
Family circumstance problems	V61.2, V61.23, V61.24, V61.25, V61.29, V61.8, V61.9
Maltreatment related	V61.11, V61.12, V61.21, V61.22, V62.83, 995.80-995.85
Life circumstance problems	V62.xx (excluding V62.6, V62.83)
Mental, behavioral problems, substance abuse counseling	V40.xx (excluding V40.0, V40.1), V65.42

Source: From "Mental Disorders and Mental Health Problems, Active Component, U.S. Armed Forces, 2000- 2011," Medical Surveillance Monthly Report, 19(6), June 2012.

Figure A-1. Codes Used by the Medical Surveillance Monthly Report and the Armed Forces Medical Examiners to Track Mental Health Diagnoses and Other Behavioral Health Concerns.

APPENDIX B. LEGISLATION

National Defense Authorization for Fiscal Year 2013

The National Defense Authorization Act for Fiscal Year 2013 (P.L. 112-239) contained several sections addressing military mental health issues, including:

- *Section 580* required the Secretary of Defense, acting through the Under Secretary of Defense for Personnel and Readiness, to establish within the Office of the Secretary of Defense a position with responsibility for oversight of all suicide prevention and resilience programs of DOD and each of the military departments.
- *Section 581* amended Chapter 1007 of Title 10, United States Code, to codify the Suicide Prevention and Community Health and Response Program for National Guard and Reserve component members, to require the Secretary of Defense to provide training on suicide prevention, resilience, and community healing and response at Yellow Ribbon Reintegration Program events and activities, to move the program from within the Office for Reintegration Programs to the Office of the Secretary of Defense, and to repeal subsection (i) of Section 582 of the National Defense Authorization Act for Fiscal Year 2008 (10 U.S.C. 10101 note). The program would terminate on October 1, 2017.
- *Section 582* required the Secretary of Defense, acting through the Under Secretary of Defense for Personnel and Readiness, to develop within the Department of Defense a comprehensive policy on the prevention of suicide among servicemembers.
- *Section 583* required the Secretary of the Army to conduct a study of resilience programs within the Army that would draw upon professionally accepted measurements and assessments to evaluate the impact of these programs.
- *Section 703* amended Section 1074m(a) of Title 10, United States Code, to align mandatory post-deployment person-to-person mental health assessments for certain servicemembers with other existing health assessments by changing the required assessment period from between 180 days after deployment to 1 year after deployment, to between 180 days after deployment to 18 months after deployment.

- *Section 706* authorized the Secretary of Defense to carry out a pilot program to enhance the efforts of DOD in research, treatment, education, and outreach on mental health, substance use disorders, and traumatic brain injury in members of the National Guard and Reserves, their family members, and their caregivers through agreements with community partners.
- *Section 723* required the Secretary of Defense and the Secretary of Veterans Affairs to jointly enter into a memorandum of understanding providing for the sharing between departments of the results of examinations and other records on members of the Armed Forces that are retained and maintained with respect to the medical tracking system for members deployed overseas.
- *Section 724* required the Secretary of Defense and the Secretary of Veterans Affairs to jointly enter into a memorandum of understanding providing for certain members of the Armed Forces to volunteer or be considered for employment as peer counselors under certain peer support counseling programs carried out by the Secretary of Veterans Affairs.
- *Section 725* required the Secretary of Defense to provide for the translation of research on the diagnosis and treatment of mental health conditions into policy on medical practices.
- *Section 726* required the Secretary of Veterans Affairs to develop and implement a comprehensive set of measures to assess mental health care services provided by the Department of Veterans Affairs.
- *Section 727* authorized the Secretary of Veterans Affairs to provide counseling and mental health services to certain members of the Armed Forces and their family members at vet centers.
- *Section 729* required the Secretary of Veterans Affairs to carry out a national program of outreach to societies, community organizations, nonprofit organizations, and government entities in order to recruit mental health providers to provide mental health care services for the VA on a part-time, without compensation basis.
- *Section 730* amended Section 1720F(j) of Title 38, United States Code, to require the Secretary of Veterans Affairs to establish and carry out a peer support counseling program as a part of the existing comprehensive program designed to reduce the incidence of suicide among veterans.

NATIONAL DEFENSE AUTHORIZATION ACT FOR FISCAL YEAR 2012

The National Defense Authorization Act for Fiscal Year 2012 (P.L. 112-81) contained provisions that addressed military mental health issues:

- *Section 703* authorized the Secretary of Defense to provide to any Reserve member performing inactive-duty training during scheduled unit training assemblies access to mental health assessments with a licensed mental health professional who would be available for referrals during duty hours at the principal duty location of the member's unit. The provision further required each Reserve member participating in annual training or individual training to have access to behavioral health support programs.
- *Section 711* directed the Secretary of Defense to prescribe and maintain regulations relating to commanding officer and supervisor referrals of members for mental health evaluations. The provision required that these regulations seek to eliminate any perceived stigma associated with seeking and receiving mental health services. The provision further outlined procedures for mental health evaluations, and prohibited using such referrals to retaliate against whistleblowers.
- *Section 723* required the Secretary of Defense to report to the defense and appropriations committees assessing the benefits of neuroimaging in an effort to identify and improve the diagnosis of PTSD.[117]
- *Section 724* directed the Secretary of Defense to report to the defense and appropriations committees on the implementation of DOD policy related to the management of concussion and mild traumatic brain injury in the deployed setting.[118]

National Defense Authorization Act for Fiscal Year 2011

The Ike Skelton National Defense Authorization Act for Fiscal Year 2011 (P.L. 111-383) contained provisions that addressed military mental health issues:

- *Section 712* required the current DOD medical tracking system for members deployed overseas to include the use of pre- and post-deployment medical examinations and health reassessments to (1) reflect the medical condition of members before their deployment; (2) record any changes to their condition during their deployment; and (3) identify health concerns, including mental health concerns, that may become manifest several months following their deployment. The provision further required that these medical records include information on the prescription and administration of psychotropic medications.

- *Section 713* provided license requirements for health care professionals who are members of the National Guard performing training or duty in response to an actual or potential disaster while operating in their state role.
- *Section 722* required the Secretary of Defense to (1) develop and implement a comprehensive policy on consistent automated neurological cognitive assessments of members before and after deployment; and (2) revise the policy on a periodic basis in accordance with experience and evolving best practice guidelines.
- *Section 723* directed the military department Secretaries to assess and report on the incidence of PTSD by military occupation. It further required the Secretary of Defense to ensure that all such assessments, findings, plans, and reports are transmitted to the centers of excellence for the treatment and prevention of PTSD and traumatic brain injury, as established under the NDAA for Fiscal Year 2008.[119]
- *Section 724* requires the Secretary to prescribe regulations concerning requirements that mental health counselors must meet in order to practice independently under TRICARE.

S.Rept. 111-201 requested the Secretary of Defense to submit a report on cognitive rehabilitation therapy for TBI. In response, on April 30, 2012, the Under Secretary of Defense for Personnel and Readiness submitted a report to Congress entitled "Cognitive Rehabilitation Therapy for Traumatic Brain Injury."[120]

National Defense Authorization Act for Fiscal Year 2010

The National Defense Authorization Act for Fiscal Year 2010 (P.L. 111-84) contained provisions that addressed military mental health issues:

- *Section 521* authorized the Secretary of each military department to detail officers as students at accredited schools of psychology in the United States for training leading to a degree of Doctor of Philosophy in clinical psychology.
- *Section 595* amended the NDAA for Fiscal Year 2008 to direct the Office for Reintegration Programs (part of the Yellow Ribbon Reintegration Program under such act) to establish a program to provide National Guard and Reserve members and their families, and assist local communities, with training in suicide prevention and community healing and response to suicide.
- *Section 596* directed the Secretary of Defense to (1) conduct a comprehensive review and assessment of DOD programs and activities for the prevention, diagnosis, and treatment of substance abuse disorders in members, as well as DOD policies relating to the disposition of substance abuse offenders in the Armed Forces; (2) report findings and recommendations to the defense committees; and (3) submit to the defense and appropriations committees a plan for the improvement and enhancement of such programs, activities, and policies. The section also requires such plan to include a comprehensive DOD statement of policy, mechanisms to ensure the availability of services and treatment as well as the prevention and reduction of substance abuse disorders, and specific instructions on the prevention, diagnosis, and treatment of substance abuse in members. It also requires confidentiality for members with respect to treatment. This section also directs the (1) Secretary of Defense to provide for an independent study on substance use disorders programs for servicemembers by the Institute of Medicine of the National Academy of Sciences or other independent entity; and (2) the results of this report must be reported to the Secretary of Defense and the defense and appropriations committees.
- *Section 708* directed the Secretary of Defense to issue guidance for the provision of a person-to-person mental health assessment for each member deployed in connection with a contingency operation within specified periods before and following deployment. It excludes from assessment requirements members determined not to have been subjected or exposed to operational risk factors during such deployment.

- *Section 712* directed the Secretary of Defense to (1) report to the defense and appropriations committees on the implementation of DOD policy guidance regarding deployment-limiting psychiatric conditions and medications; and (2) establish and implement a policy for the use of psychotropic medications for deployed members.
- *Section 714* directed each military department secretary to increase by a specified amount the number of active-duty mental health care personnel authorized for that department. Requires the Secretary of Defense to (1) report to the defense and appropriations committees on the appropriate number of such personnel required to meet the mental health care needs of members; (2) develop and implement a plan to significantly increase the number of such personnel by the end of FY2013; and (3) report to such committees on the feasibility and advisability of establishing one or more military mental health specialties for officers or enlisted members in order to better meet the mental health care needs of members and their families. In response to these reporting requirements, DOD submitted a report entitled "Mental Health Personnel Required to Meet Mental Health Care Needs of Service Members, Retired Members, and Dependents."[121]
- *Section 715* required the Secretary of Defense to (1) conduct a study on the management of medications for physically and psychologically wounded members; and (2) report study results to the defense committees.[122]
- *Section 722* directed the Secretary of Defense to (1) conduct a comprehensive review of the mental health care and counseling services available to dependent children of members; (2) report review results to the defense committees; and (3) develop and implement a comprehensive plan for improvements in access to quality mental health care and counseling services for military children.
- *Section 723* required the Secretary of Defense to (1) provide for a clinical trial to assess the efficacy of cognitive rehabilitative therapy for members and former members who have been diagnosed with a traumatic brain injury incurred in the line of duty in Operations Iraqi Freedom or Enduring Freedom and are referred for such therapy; and (2) provide an initial and final assessment report to the defense and appropriations committees.[123]

- *Section 726* directed the Secretary of Defense to provide for a study on the treatment of PTSD, to be conducted by the Institute of Medicine of the National Academy of Sciences or other independent entity.

National Defense Authorization Act for Fiscal Year 2009

The Duncan Hunter National Defense Authorization Act for Fiscal Year 2009 (P.L. 110-417) contained provisions that addressed military mental health issues:

- *Section 733* required DOD to establish a task force to examine matters relating to the prevention of suicide by members of the Armed Forces. The task force was required to report to the Secretary recommendations on a comprehensive policy designed to prevent such suicides.

In response to language in H.Rept. 110-652 to the National Defense Authorization Act for Fiscal Year 2009, on August 26, 2010, DOD reported to Congress on the possibility for providing a referral for a second opinion to potentially suicidal servicemembers in combat. This report stated that DOD has decided not to develop a policy to mandate consultation or second opinion for suicidal patients in theater.[124]

In response to additional language in the same House report, on June 2, 2009, DOD reported to Congress on DOD progress on suicide prevention. The report stated that the RAND National Defense Research Institute as well as the DOD Suicide Prevention Task Force were undertaking evaluations of matters related to suicide prevention.[125]

National Defense Authorization Act for Fiscal Year 2008

The National Defense Authorization Act for Fiscal Year 2008 (P.L. 110-181) contained provisions that addressed military mental health issues:

- *Section 708* included mental health care within the definition of "health care" under the TRICARE program. It also required a report from the Secretary of Defense to the defense committees on the adequacy of access to mental health services under the TRICARE program.

- *Section 716* required the Secretary to conduct a comprehensive review of (1) the need for gender- and ethnic group-specific mental health treatment and services for members; and (2) the efficacy and adequacy of existing gender- and ethnic group-specific mental health treatment programs and services for members.
- *Section 717* directed the Secretary of Defense to (1) establish criteria that licensed or certified mental health counselors must meet in order to independently provide care to TRICARE beneficiaries; (2) contract for an independent study of the credentials, preparation, and training of such individuals; and (3) report study results to the defense committees.
- *Section 1621* required the Secretary to establish in DOD a center of excellence in the prevention, diagnosis, mitigation, treatment, and rehabilitation of (1) TBI; (2) PTSD; and (3) military eye injuries
- *Section 1661* directed the Secretary to enter into an agreement with the National Academy of Sciences (NAS) for a study on the physical and mental health and other readjustment needs of members and former members who deployed in Operations Iraqi Freedom or Enduring Freedom (and their families) as a result of such deployment. Requires the (1) NAS to report to the Secretaries and the defense and appropriations committees upon the completion of each of the two phases of such study; and (2) Secretaries to develop a final DOD-VA response to such findings and recommendations.
- *Section 1634* required a joint report from the Secretaries to the defense committees on DOD-VA changes to ensure that traumatic brain injury victims receive a medical designation concomitant with such injury, rather than a designation which assigns a generic classification such as "organic psychiatric disorder."[126]

National Defense Authorization Act for Fiscal Year 2007

The John Warner National Defense Authorization Act for Fiscal Year 2007 (P.L. 109-364) contained provisions that addressed military mental health issues:

- *Section 721* directed the Secretary of Defense to (1) conduct a 15-year longitudinal study on the effects of traumatic brain injury incurred by members of the Armed Forces in Operations Iraqi Freedom and Enduring Freedom; and (2) provide periodic and final reports to Congress on study results.
- *Section 735* amended the NDAA for Fiscal Year 2006 to require the task force on mental health established under such act to consider, as part of its assessment of DOD mental health services provided to military personnel, the specific needs of members deployed in Operations Iraqi Freedom or Enduring Freedom upon their return from deployment.
- *Section 738* required additional elements for pre-deployment and post-deployment medical examinations, including current treatment and an assessment of traumatic brain injury, and provides criteria for referral for further evaluation. It also directs the Secretary of Defense to prescribe minimum mental health standards for eligibility of a member for deployment to a combat or contingency operation. Requires the (1) Comptroller General to conduct a study of, and report to the defense committees on, the implementation of the requirements of this section; and (2) the Secretary of Defense to implement the requirements and report to such committees on such implementation.
- *Section 741* directed the Secretary to carry out no less than three one-year pilot projects to evaluate the efficacy of various approaches to improving the capability of the military and civilian health care system to provide early diagnosis and treatment of post-traumatic stress disorder (PTSD) and other mental health conditions. Requires one of such projects to be (1) designed to evaluate diagnostic and treatment approaches for use by primary care providers to improve the diagnosis and treatment of PTSD; (2) focused on members of the National Guard or Reserve located more than 40 miles from a military medical facility, and whose personnel are served primarily by civilian community health resources; and (3) designed to provide outreach to family members on PTSD and other mental health conditions.
- *Section 744* required the Secretary to establish within DOD a panel to develop curricula for training family members in the provision of care and assistance to members and former members with traumatic brain injuries. It designated this panel as the Traumatic Brain Injury Family Caregiver Panel.

National Defense Authorization Act for Fiscal Year 2006

The National Defense Authorization Act for Fiscal Year 2006 (P.L. 109-163) contained provisions that addressed military mental health issues:

- *Section 594* required a member's pre-separation counseling to include information concerning (1) the availability of mental health services and the treatment of post-traumatic stress disorder (PTSD), anxiety, depression, suicide, and other mental health conditions associated with service in the Armed Forces; (2) veterans' training and hiring priorities; (3) veterans' small business ownership and entrepreneurship programs; (4) employment and reemployment rights; (5) veterans' preference in federal employment; (6) available housing counseling assistance; and (7) a description of veterans' health care and other benefits.
- *Section 721* required the Secretary to develop a program to improve awareness of the availability of mental health services for, and warning signs about mental health problems in, dependents of members who served or will serve in a combat theater during the previous or next 60 days. It also directs the Secretary to (1) carry out a pilot project to evaluate the efficacy of various approaches to improving the capability of the military and civilian health care systems to provide early diagnosis and treatment of PTSD and other mental health conditions; and (2) report to the defense and appropriations committees on the project.
- *Section 722* authorized the Secretary to carry out pilot projects on improving the early diagnosis and treatment of PTSD and other mental health conditions. Authorizes at least one such project at a National Guard or Reserve facility located at least 40 miles from a military medical facility and whose personnel are served primarily by civilian community health resources.
- *Section 723* required (1) the Secretary to establish within DOD a task force to examine matters relating to mental health and the Armed Forces; (2) the task force to report to the Secretary, including an assessment of, and recommendations for improving, mental health care provided by the military departments; (3) the task force to report to the Secretary on all activities undertaken under this section; and (4)

the latter report to be transmitted to the defense and veterans' committees.[127]

National Defense Authorization Act for Fiscal Year 2005

The Ronald W. Reagan National Defense Authorization Act for Fiscal Year 2005 (P.L. 108-375) contained provisions that addressed military mental health issues:

- *Section 723* required the Comptroller General to study, and report to Congress on, mental health services available to members of the Armed Forces, including: (1) the availability and effectiveness of existing mental health treatment and screening resources; and (2) obstacles preventing members and their families from obtaining needed services.

End Notes

[1] Kessler RC, Chiu WT, Demler O, Walters EE. Prevalence, severity, and comorbidity of twelve-month DSM-IV disorders in the National Comorbidity Survey Replication (NCS-R). Archives of General Psychiatry, 2005 Jun;62(6):617-27.

[2] "Mental Disorders and Mental Health Problems, Active Component, U.S. Armed Forces, 2000-2011," Medical Surveillance Monthly Report, vol. 19, no. 6 (June 2012), pp. 11-17.

[3] Mental Disorders and Mental Health Problems, Active Component, U.S. Armed Forces, 2000-2011," Medical Surveillance Monthly Report, vol. 19, no. 6 (June 2012), pp. 11-17.

[4] "Mental Disorders and Mental Health Problems, Active Component, U.S. Armed Forces, 2000-2011," Medical Surveillance Monthly Report, vol. 19, no. 6 (June 2012), pp. 11-17.

[5] Defense and Veterans Brain Injury Center, "DOD Worldwide Numbers for TBI." http://www.dvbic.org/dodworldwide-numbers-tbi

[6] Kathryn R. Marshall, Sherray L. Holland, and Kimberly S. Meyer, et al., "Mild Traumatic Brain Injury Screening, Diagnosis, and Treatment," Military Medicine, Vol. 177, No. 8:67, August 2012 Supplement, p. 67.

[7] "External Causes of Traumatic Brain Injury, 2000-2011." Monthly Surveillance Medical Report, Armed Forces Health Surveillance Center. Vol 20, No 3. p. 13.

[8] "Deaths by Suicide While on Active Duty, Active and Reserve Components, U.S. Armed Forces, 1998-2011," Medical Surveillance Monthly Report, vol. 19, no. 6 (June 2012), pp. 11-17.

[9] "Deaths by Suicide While on Active Duty, Active and Reserve Components, U.S. Armed Forces, 1998-2011," Medical Surveillance Monthly Report, vol. 19, no. 6 (June 2012), pp. 11-17.

[10] Charles W. Hoge and Carl A. Castro, "Preventing Suicides in US Service Members and Veterans: Concerns After a Decade of War," Journal of the American Medical Association, Vol. 308, no. 7 (August 15, 2012), p. 671.

[11] Charles W. Hoge and Carl A. Castro, "Preventing Suicides in US Service Members and Veterans: Concerns After a Decade of War," Journal of the American Medical Association, Vol. 308, no. 7 (August 15, 2012), p. 671; Eaton KM, Messer SC, Garvey Wilson AL, Hoge CW, "Strengthening the validity of population-based suicide rate comparisons: an illustration using U.S. military and civilian data." Suicide and Life-Threatening Behavior. April 2006, 36(2), pp. 182-91.

[12] Department of Defense Instruction (DODI) 6130.03: Accession Medical Standard.

[13] Communication from DOD official dated 9/1/2010.

[14] Department of Defense Instruction 6025.19: Individual Medical Readiness (IMR http://www.dtic.mil/whs/directives/ corres/pdf/602519p.pdf).

[15] 10 U.S.C. §1074m.

[16] Assistant Secretary of Defense for Health Affairs Memorandum, "Policy Guidance for Deployment-Limiting Psychiatric Conditions and Medications," November 7, 2006, (http://tricare.mil/tma/congressionalinformation/ downloads/200803/MedicalReadinessPlanJointMedicalReadinessOversightCommittee.pdf).

[17] 32 CFR §199.2.

[18] Program regulations are at 32 C.F.R. §199.16.

[19] Subsection 714(b)(2) of the National Defense Authorization Act for Fiscal Year 2010 (P.L. 111-84).

[20] Defense Health Program Fiscal Year (FY) 2014 Budget Estimates, p. 14. Available at http://comptroller.defense.gov/defbudget/fy2014/budget_justification/pdfs/09_Defense_ Health_Program/ FY2014_DHP_Budget_Estimates_Vol_1.pdf.

[21] Department of Defense and Department of Veterans Affairs, VA/DOD Clinical Practice Guideline For Management of Post-Traumatic Stress, available at http://www.healthquality.va.gov/Post_Traumatic_Stress_Disorder_PTSD.asp.

[22] Department of Defense and Department of Veterans Affairs, Management of Concussion-mild TBI available at http://www.healthquality.va.gov/management_of_concussion_mtbi.asp.

[23] Department of Defense and Department of Veterans Affairs, Management of Major Depressive Disorder, available at http://www.healthquality.va.gov/Major_Depressive_ Disorder_ MDD_Clinical_Practice_Guideline.asp.

[24] Department of Defense and Department of Veterans Affairs, Management of Substance Abuse Disorder, available at http://www.healthquality.va.gov/Substance_Use_Disorder_SUD.asp.

[25] Department of Defense Instruction number 6490.08 "Command Notification Requirements to Dispel Stigma in Providing Mental Health Care to Service Members," available at http://www.dtic.mil/whs/directives/corres/pdf/ 649008p.pdf.

[26] "Selected Mental Health Disorders Among Active Component Members, U.S. Armed Forces, 2007-2010." Monthly Surveillance Medical Report, Armed Forces Health Surveillance Center. Vol 17, No 11. Supplemental Report. p. 11.

[27] Report of the Joint Mental Health Advisory Team 7 (J-MHAT 7) Operation Enduring Freedom 2010 Afghanistan, February 22, 2011, p. 33.

[28] A 2011 RAND study identified 77 such programs. For the full list, see Meredith, Lisa et al, "Promoting Psychological Resilience in the U.S. Military," 2011, appendix C. The RAND Corporation, 2011. Available at http://www.rand.org/content/dam/rand/pubs/monographs/ 2011/RAND_MG996.pdf.

[29] Meredith, Lisa et al, Promoting Psychological Resilience in the U.S. Military, 2011, appendix C. The RAND Corporation, 2011, p. 75. Available at http://www.rand.org/content/dam/rand/pubs/monographs/2011/ RAND_MG996.pdf.

[30] Ramchand, Rajeev, Joie Acosta, Rachel M. Burns, Lisa H. Jaycox and Christopher G. Pernin. The War Within: Preventing Suicide in the U.S. Military, The RAND Corporation, 2011, p. 83. Available at http://www.rand.org/pubs/ monographs/MG953.

[31] Ibid, p. 118.

[32] Nick Simeone, "DOD Health Official Updates Status of PTSD, TBI Care," American Forces Press Service, January 13, 2013, http://www.defense.gov/news/newsarticle.aspx?id = 119020.

[33] Institute of Medicine, "Treatment for Posttraumatic Stress Disorder in Military and Veteran Populations: Initial Assessment." July 13, 2012. http://www.iom.edu/Reports/2012/ Treatment-for-Posttraumatic-Stress-Disorder-inMilitary-and-Veteran-Populations-Initial-Assessment.aspx.

[34] Department of Defense, "Report to Congress on the Institute of Medicine Report "Treatment for Posttraumatic Stress Disorder in Military and Veteran Populations: Initial Assessment" In Accordance with Section 726 of the National Defense Authorization Act For Fiscal Year 2010, pp. 5-6, January 2013. Available at http://www.tricare.mil/tma/ congressionalinformation/downloads/Independent%20Study%20on%20Post-Traumatic%20Stress%20Disorder%20%28PTSD%29%20Efforts.pdf.

[35] Ramchand, Rajeev, Joie Acosta, Rachel M. Burns, Lisa H. Jaycox and Christopher G. Pernin, The War Within: Preventing Suicide in the U.S. Military. Santa Monica, CA: RAND Corporation, 2011. Available at http://www.rand.org/pubs/monographs/MG953.

[36] DOD Task Force on the Prevention of Suicide by Members of the Armed Forces, "The Challenge and the Promise: Strengthening the Force, Preventing Suicide and Saving Lives," August 2010. Available at http://www.health.mil/dhb/ downloads/Suicide%20Prevention%20Task%20Force%20final%20report%208-23-10.pdf.

[37] Military Health Advisory Team reports are available at http://www.armymedicine.army.mil/ reports/mhat/mhat.html.

[38] See Joint Mental Health Advisory Team 7 (J-MHAT 7) Operation Enduring Freedom 2010 Afghanistan, February 22 2011, p. 95. Available at http://www.armymedicine.army.mil/ reports/mhat/mhat_vii/J_MHAT_7.pdf.

[39] Executive Order 13625 "Improving Access to Mental Health Services for Veterans, Service Members, and Military Families," August 31, 2012.

[40] Institute of Medicine, "Treatment for Posttraumatic Stress Disorder in Military and Veteran Populations: Initial Assessment." July 13, 2012, p. 375 http://www.iom.edu/Reports/2012/ Treatment-for-Posttraumatic-Stress-Disorder-inMilitary-and-Veteran-Populations-Initial-Assessment.aspx.

[41] Institute of Medicine "Report Brief," March 26, 2013, p. 1. Available at http://www.iom.edu/Reports/2013/Returning-Home-from-Iraq-and-Afghanistan/Report-Brief 032613.aspx.

[42] For more information the Armed Forces Health Surveillance Center's standard methodologies used for routine surveillance and reporting of medical cases, please see their methodological guide, located at http://www.afhsc.mil/ viewDocument?file=CaseDefs/Web_ Introduction_ Final_9Mar11.pdf. The descriptions of the criteria for inclusion of mental health cases are found at http://www.afhsc.mil/viewDocument?file=CaseDefs/ Web_12_ MENTAL%20 HEALTH_SEPT12.pdf.

[43] Department of Veterans Affairs, VetPop11 projection model. https://www.va.gov/ vetdata/Veteran_Population.asp.

[44] Department of Defense report, see http://siadapp.dmdc.osd.mil/personnel/MILITARY/history/hst1109.pdf

[45] DOD uses the Diagnostic and Statistical Manual of Mental Disorders (DSM) – IV text revision published by the American Psychiatric Association in 2000 and frequently referred to as "DSM-IV-TR." The 5th edition, the DSM-V , was published on May 18, 2013, superseding the DSM-IV-TR.

[46] Adapted from Congressional Budget Office, "The Veterans Health Administration's Treatment of PTSD and Traumatic Brain Injury Among Recent Combat Veterans." February 2012, p. 23. http://www.cbo.gov/publication/ 42969.

[47] Analysis by CRS. Data from "Selected Mental Health Disorders Among Active Component Members, U.S. Armed Forces, 2007-2010," Monthly Surveillance Medical Report, Armed Forces Health Surveillance Center. Vol. 17, No. 11, Supplemental Report. p. 3.

[48] The incidence figures presented above are of PTSD among deployed and non-deployed servicemembers diagnosed with PTSD in the military medical system. Therefore, these incidence numbers are likely to be lower than the true incidence rate, as they will not capture servicemembers who either do not seek psychological health treatment or who do not seek it within the military medical system. Service members who are deployed in connection with a contingency operation are required to receive periodic person-to-person mental health assessments. While these screenings may capture symptoms of PTSD, they are not in themselves sufficient to establish a diagnosis of PTSD.

[49] Brett T. Litz and William E. Schlenger, "PTSD in Service Members and New Veterans of the Iraq and Afghanistan Wars: A Bibliography and Critique," PTSD Research Quarterly, Vol. 20 No. 1 (Winter 2009). p. 3.

[50] Milliken, C. S., Auchterlonie, J. L., & Hoge, C. W. Longitudinal assessment of mental health problems among active and reserve component soldiers returning from the Iraq War. Journal of the American Medical Association, 298, 20078, pp. 2141-2148.

[51] Schell, T. L., and Marshall, G. N. (2008), "Survey of individuals previously deployed for OEF/OIF," in T. Tanielian and L. H. Jaycox (Eds.), Invisible Wounds of War: Psychological and Cognitive Injuries, Their Consequences, and Services to Assist Recovery, pp. 87-115, Santa Monica, CA: RAND Center for Military Health Policy Research.

[52] Kessler, R.C., Berglund, P., Delmer, O., Jin, R., Merikangas, K.R., and Walters, E.E. (2005), "Lifetime Prevalence and Age-of-Onset Distributions of DSM-IV Disorders in the National Comorbidity Survey Replication," Archives of General Psychiatry, 62(6): 593-602. Data from the the National Comorbidity Survey Replication (NCS-R), conducted between February 2001 and April 2003, based upon interviews of a nationally representative sample of Americans aged 18 years and older. The lifetime prevalence of PTSD among men was 3.6% and among women was 9.7%.

[53] Kessler, R.C., Chiu, W.T., Demler, O., Merikangas, K.R., and Walters, E.E. (2005), "Prevalence, Severity, and Comorbidity of 12-Month DSM-IV Disorders in the National Comorbidity Survey Replication," Archives of General Psychiatry, 62(6): 617-627. The twelve-month prevalence was 1.8% among men and 5.2% among women. National Comorbidity Survey (2005), NCS-R Appendix Tables: Table 1. Lifetime Prevalence of DSM-IV/WMH-CIDI Disorders by Sex and Cohort. Table 2. Twelve-Month Prevalence of DSM-IV/WMH-CIDI Disorders by Sex and Cohort. Available at http://www.hcp.med.harvard.edu/ncs/publications.php.

[54] CRS communication with Dr. Michael Carino, Army Office of the Surgeon General, December 13, 2012. Data source is the Defense Medical Surveillance System (DMSS).

[55] Phillips, C.J., Leardman, C.A., Gumbs, G.R., and Smith, B., "Risk Factors For Posttraumatic Stress Disorder Among Deployed US Male Marines," BMC Psychiatry, 2010; 10: 52, and Sandweiss, D.A., Slymen, D.J., Leardman, C.A., et al., "Preinjury Psychiatric Status, Injury Severity, and Postdeployment Posttraumatic Stress Disorder," Archives of General Psychiatry, 2011, 68: pp. 496-504. Cited in Herman, Barbara A., Brian Shiner, Matthew J. Friedman, "Epidemiology and Prevention of Combat-Related Post-Traumatic Stress in OEF/OIF/OND Service Members." Military Medicine, 177, 8:1, p. 3.

[56] Pietrzak, R.H., Johnson, D.C., Goldstein, M.B., et al., "Psychosocial Buffers of Traumatic Stress, Depressive Symptoms, and Psychosocial Difficulties in Veterans of Operations Enduring Freedom and Iraqi Freedom: The Role of Resilience, Unit Support, and Postdeployment Social Support," Journal of Affective Disorders, 2010; 120, pp. 188-192. Cited in Herman, Barbara A., Brian Shiner, Matthew J. Friedman, "Epidemiology and Prevention of Combat-Related Post-Traumatic Stress in OEF/OIF/OND Service Members." Military Medicine, 177, 8:1, p. 3.

[57] Polusny, M.A., Erbes, C.R., and Murdoch, M., et al., "Prospective Risk Factors for New-Onset Post-Traumatic Stress Disorder in National Guard Soldiers Deployed to Iraq," Psychological Medicine 2011, (41), pp. 687-698; and Riviere, L.A., Kendall-Robbins, A., and McGurk, D., et al., "Coming Home May Hurt: Risk Factors for Mental Ill Health in US Reservists After Deployment in Iraq," British Journal of Psychiatry 2011 (198), pp. 136-142. Cited in Herman, Barbara A., Brian Shiner, and Matthew J. Friedman, "Epidemiology and Prevention of Combat-Related Post-Traumatic Stress in OEF/OIF/OND Service Members," Military Medicine, 177, 8:1, p. 3.

[58] American Psychiatric Association, Diagnostic and Statistical Manual of Mental Disorders, Fourth Edition, Text Revision (Washington, DC: American Psychiatric Association, 2000), pp. 191-199.

[59] American Psychiatric Association, Diagnostic and Statistical Manual of Mental Disorders, Fourth Edition, Text Revision (Washington, DC: American Psychiatric Association, 2000), p. 197.

[60] "Alcohol-related Diagnoses, Active Component, U.S. Armed Forces, 2001-2011." Medical Surveillance Monthly Report, 18(10), October 2011. pp. 9-11.

[61] "Surveillance Snapshot: Recurrent Medical Encounters Associated with Alcohol Abuse-Related Diagnostic Codes, Active Compontent, U.S. Armed Forces, 2001-2010," Medical Surveillance Monthly Report, 19(2), February 2012, p. 23.

[62] "Alcohol-Related Diagnoses, Active Component, U.S. Armed Forces, 2001-2011," Medical Surveillance Monthly Report, 18(10), October 2011. p. 10.

[63] "Alcohol-Related Diagnoses, Active Component, U.S. Armed Forces, 2001-2011," Medical Surveillance Monthly Report, 18(10), October 2011. p. 9.

[64] Servies, Tammy, Zheng Hu, and Angelia Eick-Cost, et al., "Substance Use Disorders in the U.S. Armed Forces, 2000-2011," Medical Surveillance Monthly Report, 19(11) November 2012, p. 11.

[65] Servies, Tammy, Zheng Hu, and Angelia Eick-Cost, et al., "Substance Use Disorders in the U.S. Armed Forces, 2000-2011," Medical Surveillance Monthly Report, 19(11) November 2012, p. 15.

[66] Sirratt, Deborah, Alfred Ozanian, and Barbara Traenkner, "Epidemiology and Prevention of Substance Abuse Disorders in the Military," Military Medicine, 177, August Supplement 2012, p. 23.

[67] Ronald C. Kessler, Patricia Berglund, and Olga Demler, et al., "The Epidemology of Major Depressive Disorder: Results from the National Comorbidity Survey Replication (NCS-R),"

Journal of the American Medical Association, vol. 289, no. 23 (June 18, 2003), pp. 3095-3105.

[68] Gaderman, et. al., "Prevalence of DSM-IV Major Depression Among U.S. Military Personnel," Military Medicine, Vol. 177, August Supplement 2012.

[69] Data from "Selected Mental Health Disorders Among Active Component Members, U.S. Armed Forces, 2007- 2010," Monthly Surveillance Medical Report, Armed Forces Health Surveillance Center. Vol 17, No 11. Supplemental Report. p. 3.

[70] Data from "Selected Mental Health Disorders Among Active Component Members, U.S. Armed Forces, 2007- 2010," Monthly Surveillance Medical Report, Armed Forces Health Surveillance Center. Vol 17, No 11. Supplemental Report. p. 3.

[71] American Psychiatric Association, Diagnostic and Statistical Manual of Mental Disorders, Fourth Edition, Text Revision (Washington, DC: American Psychiatric Association, 2000), pp. 679-683.

[72] Analysis by CRS. Data provided by the Armed Forces Health Surveillance Center, expanded from the data presented in "Mental Disorders And Mental Health Problems, Active Component, U.S. Armed Forces, 2000-2011," Medical Surveillance Monthly Report, 19(6), June 2012.

[73] Skopp, N., Trofimovich, L., Grimes, J., et al, "Relations between suicide and traumatic brain injury, psychiatric diagnoses, and relationship problems, active component, U.S. Armed Forces, 2001-2009, Military Medical Surveillance Report, 19(2), 2012, pp. 473-481.

[74] Adapted from Congressional Budget Office, "The Veterans Health Administration's Treatment of PTSD and Traumatic Brain Injury Among Recent Combat Veterans." February 2012. p. 24.

[75] Kathryn R. Marshall, Sherray L. Holland, and Kimberly S. Meyer, et al., "Mild Traumatic Brain Injury Diagnosis, and Treatment," Military Medicine, Vol. 177, No. 8, August 2012 Supplement, p. 67.

[76] Defense and Veterans Brain Injury Center, "DoD Worldwide Numbers for TBI." Available at http://www.dvbic.org/ dod-worldwide-numbers-tbi.

[77] Kathryn R. Marshall, Sherray L. Holland, and Kimberly S. Meyer, et al., "Mild Traumatic Brain Injury Screening, Diagnosis, and Treatment," Military Medicine, Vol. 177, No. 8, August 2012 Supplement, p. 70.

[78] Kathryn R. Marshall, Sherray L. Holland, and Kimberly S. Meyer, et al., "Mild Traumatic Brain Injury Screening, Diagnosis, and Treatment," Military Medicine, Vol. 177, No. 8:67, August 2012 Supplement, p. 70.

[79] Maj. Scot A. Marshall and Ronald G. Riechters II, "Diagnosis and Management of Moderate and Severe Traumatic Brain Injury Sustained in Combat," Military Medicine Vol. 177, No. 8, August 2012 Supplement, p. 76.

[80] Kathryn R. Marshall, Sherray L. Holland, and Kimberly S. Meyer, et al., "Mild Traumatic Brain Injury Screening, Diagnosis, and Treatment," Military Medicine, Vol. 177, No. 8, August 2012 Supplement, p. 67.

[81] "External Causes of Traumatic Brain Injury, 2000-2011," Monthly Surveillance Medical Report, Armed Forces Health Surveillance Center, Vol. 20, No. 3, p. 13.

[82] DTM 09-033 and DODI 6490.1.

[83] "External Causes of Traumatic Brain Injury, 2000-2011," Monthly Surveillance Medical Report, Armed Forces Health Surveillance Center, Vol. 20, No. 3, p. 13.

[84] Kathryn R. Marshall, Sherray L. Holland, and Kimberly S. Meyer, et al., "Mild Traumatic Brain Injury Screening, Diagnosis, and Treatment," Military Medicine, vol. Vol. 177, No. 8:67, August 2012 Supplement, p. 67.

85 Kathryn R. Marshall, Sherray L. Holland, and Kimberly S. Meyer, et al., "Mild Traumatic Brain Injury Screening, Diagnosis, and Treatment," Military Medicine, vol. Vol. 177, No. 8:67, August 2012 Supplement, p. 68.

86 Kathryn R. Marshall, Sherray L. Holland, and Kimberly S. Meyer, et al., "Mild Traumatic Brain Injury Screening, Diagnosis, and Treatment," Military Medicine, vol. Vol. 177, No. 8:67, August 2012 Supplement, p. 68.

87 "External Causes of Traumatic Brain Injury, 2000-2011," Monthly Surveillance Medical Report, Armed Forces Health Surveillance Center. Vol. 20, No. 3, pp. 9-13.

88 Rogers and Read (2007), "Psychiatric Comorbidity Following Traumatic Brain Injury," Brain Injury 21(13): 1321- 1333, cited in Institute of Medicine, Gulf War and Health: Volume 7: Long-Term Consequences of Traumatic Brain Injury, 2008, pp. 237-263, http://www.nap.edu/catalog/12436.html.

89 Fane et al. 2004, "Psychiatric Illness Following Traumatic Brain Injury in an Adult Health Maintenance Organization Population," Archives of General Psychiatry, 61(1): 53-61, cited in Institute of Medicine, Gulf War and Health: Volume 7: Long-Term Consequences of Traumatic Brain Injury, 2008, pp. 237-263, http://www.nap.edu/catalog/ 12436.html.

90 Institute of Medicine, Gulf War and Health: Volume 7: Long-Term Consequences of Traumatic Brain Injury, 2008, pp. 277-278, http://www.nap.edu/catalog/12436.html.

91 Institute of Medicine, Gulf War and Health: Volume 7: Long-Term Consequences of Traumatic Brain Injury, 2008, p. 284, http://www.nap.edu/catalog/12436.html.

92 Institute of Medicine, Gulf War and Health: Volume 7: Long-Term Consequences of Traumatic Brain Injury, 2008, pp. 289-293, http://www.nap.edu/catalog/12436.html.

93 Institute of Medicine, Gulf War and Health: Volume 7: Long-Term Consequences of Traumatic Brain Injury, 2008, pp. 237-263, http://www.nap.edu/catalog/12436.html.

94 Institute of Medicine, Gulf War and Health: Volume 7: Long-Term Consequences of Traumatic Brain Injury, 2008, pp. 237-263, http://www.nap.edu/catalog/12436.html.

95 "Deaths by Suicide While on Active Duty, Active and Reserve Components, U.S. Armed Forces, 1998-2011," Medical Surveillance Monthly Report, Vol. 19, No. 6 (June 2012), pp. 11-17.

96 "Deaths by Suicide While on Active Duty, Active and Reserve Components, U.S. Armed Forces, 1998-2011," Medical Surveillance Monthly Report, Vol. 19, No. 6 (June 2012), pp. 11-17.

97 National Center for Telehealth & Technology, Defense Centers of Excellence for Psychological Health & Traumatic Brain Injury, Department of Defense Suicide Event Report, Calendar Year 2011 Annual Report, November 2012. "Table 2.2 CY 2011 and 2009-2010 AFMES and DMDC Demographic Data for Suicides," p. 12.

98 Charles W. Hoge and Carl A. Castro, "Preventing Suicides in U.S. Service Members and Veterans: Concerns After a Decade of War," Journal of the American Medical Association, Vol. 308, No. 7 (August 15, 2012), p. 671; Eaton, K.M., Messer, S.C., Garvey Wilson, A.L., and Hoge, C.W., "Strengthening the Validity of Population-Based Suicide Rate Comparisons: An Illustration Using U.S. Military and Civilian Data," Suicide and Life-Threatening Behaviour, April 2006, 36(2), pp. 182-91.

99 Eaton, K.M., Messer, S.C., Garvey Wilson, A.L., and Hoge, C.W., "Strengthening the Validity of Population-Based Suicide Rate Comparisons: An Illustration Using U.S. Military and Civilian Data," Suicide and Life-Threatening Behaviour, April 2006, 36(2), pp. 182-91.

100 "Deaths by Suicide While on Active Duty, Active and Reserve Components, U.S. Armed Forces, 1998-2011," Medical Surveillance Monthly Report, Vol. 19, No. 6 (June 2012), p. 10. According to the Centers for Disease Control, in 2009, the latest year for which data are

available, the suicide rate for males between 10 and 24 years of age was 11.5 per 100,000, while the suicide rate for males between 25 and 64 years of age was 25 per 100,000.100 However, because young males make up a much greater proportion of the military population than the civilian population, active duty and civilian suicide rates are not directly comparable. Suicide rates from National Suicide Statistics at a Glance. "Trends in Suicide Rates Among Males, by Age Group, United States, 1991-2009," http://www.cdc.gov/ ViolencePrevention/ suicide/statistics/trends03.html.

101 Charles W. Hoge and Carl A. Castro, "Preventing Suicides in U.S. Service Members and Veterans: Concerns After a Decade of War," Journal of the American Medical Association, Vol. 308, No. 7 (August 15, 2012), p. 671.

102 National Center for Telehealth & Technology, Defense Centers of Excellence for Psychological Health & Traumatic Brain Injury, Department of Defense Suicide Event Report, Calendar Year 2011 Annual Report, November 2012. p. 1.

103 National Center for Telehealth & Technology, Defense Centers of Excellence for Psychological Health & Traumatic Brain Injury, Department of Defense Suicide Event Report, Calendar Year 2011 Annual Report, November 2012. p. 2.

104 National Center for Telehealth & Technology, Defense Centers of Excellence for Psychological Health & Traumatic Brain Injury, Department of Defense Suicide Event Report, Calendar Year 2011 Annual Report, November 2012. p. 2.

105 James Dao, "As Military Suicides Rise, Focus Is on Private Weapons," New York Times, October 7, 2012, http://www.nytimes.com/2012/10/08/us/with-military-suicides-rising-new-policies-take-shape.html?pagewanted=all.

106 National Center for Telehealth & Technology, Defense Centers of Excellence for Psychological Health & Traumatic Brain Injury, Department of Defense Suicide Event Report, Calendar Year 2011 Annual Report, November 2012, p. 2.

107 National Center for Telehealth & Technology, Defense Centers of Excellence for Psychological Health & Traumatic Brain Injury, Department of Defense Suicide Event Report, Calendar Year 2011 Annual Report, November 2012, pp.2- 3.

108 Charles W. Hoge and Carl A. Castro, "Preventing Suicides in US Service Members and Veterans: Concerns After a Decade of War," Journal of the American Medical Association, Vol. 308, No. 7 (August 15, 2012), pp. 671-672.

109 Charles W. Hoge and Carl A. Castro, "Preventing Suicides in US Service Members and Veterans: Concerns After a Decade of War," Journal of the American Medical Association, Vol. 308, No. 7 (August 15, 2012), pp. 671-672.

110 Armed Forces Health Surveillance Center, "Associations between Repeated Deployments to OEF/OIF/OND, October 2001-December 2010, and Post-deployment Illnesses and Injuries, Active Component, U.S. Armed Forces." Medical Surveillance Monthly Report, 18(7), July 2011, pp. 2-11.

111 Armed Forces Health Surveillance Center, "Associations between Repeated Deployments to OEF/OIF/OND, October 2001-December 2010, and Post-deployment Illnesses and Injuries, Active Component, U.S. Armed Forces." Medical Surveillance Monthly Report, 18(7), July 2011, p. 6.

112 Armed Forces Health Surveillance Center, "Associations between Repeated Deployments to OEF/OIF/OND, October 2001-December 2010, and Post-deployment Illnesses and Injuries, Active Component, U.S. Armed Forces." Medical Surveillance Monthly Report, 18(7), July 2011, p.3.

113 Armed Forces Health Surveillance Center, "Associations between Repeated Deployments to OEF/OIF/OND, October 2001-December 2010, and Post-deployment Illnesses and Injuries,

Active Component, U.S. Armed Forces." Medical Surveillance Monthly Report, 18(7), July 2011, p.3.

114 Armed Forces Health Surveillance Center, "Associations between Repeated Deployments to OEF/OIF/OND, October 2001-December 2010, and Post-deployment Illnesses and Injuries, Active Component, U.S. Armed Forces." Medical Surveillance Monthly Report, 18(7), July 2011, p.3.

115 Armed Forces Health Surveillance Center, "Associations Between Repeated Deployments to Iraq (OIF/OND) and Afghanistan (OEF) and Post-deployment Illnesses and Injuries, Active Component, U.S. Armed Forces, 2003-2010," Monthly Medical Surveillance Report, 18(9), September 2011, p. 9.

116 Armed Forces Health Surveillance Center, "Associations Between Repeated Deployments to Iraq (OIF/OND) and Afghanistan (OEF) and Post-Deployment Illnesses and Injuries, Active Component, U.S. Armed Forces, 2003-2010," Monthly Medical Surveillance Report, 18(9), September 2011, p. 9.

117 See Office of the Under Secretary of Defense (Personnel and Readiness), "Report on Research and Treatment of Posttraumatic Stress Disorder," December 17, 2012. Available at http://www.tricare.mil/tma/congressionalinformation/downloads/Report%20on%20Research%20and%20Treatment%20of%20PTSD.pdf.

118 See Office of the Under Secretary of Defense (Personnel and Readiness), "Report on Memorandum Regarding Traumatic Brain Injuries" August 1, 2012. Available at http://www.tricare.mil/tma/congressionalinformation/ downloads/Report%20on%20Memorandum%20Regarding%20TBI.pdf.

119 See http://www.tricare.mil/tma/congressionalinformation/ downloads/DoD%20Study%20on%20Management%20of%20Medications%20for%20Physically%20and%20Psychologically%20 Wounded%20Members%20of%20the%20Armed%20Forces.pdf.

120 Available at http://www.tricare.mil/tma/congressionalinformation/downloads/ Cognitive%20Rehabilitation%20Therapy%20for%20Traumatic%20Brain%20Injury.pdf.

121 Assistant Secretary of Defense (Health Affairs), February 2011, http://www.tricare.mil/tma/congressionalinformation/downloads/PlanIncreaseMentalHealthCapabilitiesDoD.pdf.

122 DOD's response to this requirement is available at http://www.tricare.mil/tma/congressional information/downloads/ DoD%20Study%20on%20Management%20of%20Medications%20for%20Physically%20and%20Psychologically%20 Wounded%20Members%20of%20the%20Armed%20Forces.pdf.

123 DOD's response to this requirement is available at http://tricare.mil/tma/congressional information/downloads/Report%20to%20Congress%20on%20Clinical%20Trial%20on%20Cognitive%20Rehabilitative%20Therapy.pdf.

124 Department of Defense, Suicide Prevention in the Armed Forces: Study on Referral for Second Option, H.Rept. 110-652 of the National Defense Authorization Act for Fiscal Year 2009, February 2010, http://www.tricare.mil/tma/ congressionalinformation/downloads/ 201063/Suicide%20Prevention%20in%20the%20Armed%20Forces.pdf.

125 Department of Defense, Progress on Suicide Prevention, H.Rept. 110-652 of the National Defense Act for Fiscal 2009, May 2009, http://www.tricare.mil/tma/congressional information/downloads/201063/ Suicide%20Prevention%20in%20the%20Armed%20Forces%20-%20FY09.pdf.

126 DOD's response is available at http://www.tricare.mil/tma/congressional information/ downloads/Reports%20Section%201634%28b%29.pdf.

[127] DOD responded with a report entitled "An Achievable Vision: Report of the Department of Defense Task Force on Mental Health," in 2007.

In: Post-Traumatic Stress and Mental Health … ISBN: 978-1-62948-403-7
Editor: Jeffrey N. Lentz

Chapter 2

VA Health Care: VA Spends Millions on Post-Traumatic Stress Disorder Research and Incorporates Research Outcomes into Guidelines and Policy for Post-Traumatic Stress Disorder Services*

United States Government Accountability Office

Abbreviations

CPG	clinical practice guideline
CSP	Cooperative Studies Program
DOD	Department of Defense
Handbook	Uniform Mental Health Services in VA Medical Centers and Clinics handbook
ORD	Office of Research and Development
PTSD	post-traumatic stress disorder
VA	Department of Veterans Affairs

* This is an edited, reformatted and augmented version of The United States Government Accountability Office publication, Report to the Ranking Member, Subcommittee on Health, Committee on Veterans' Affairs, House of Representatives, GAO-11-32, dated January 2011.

Why GAO Did This Study

In addition to providing health care to veterans, the Department of Veterans Affairs (VA) funds research that focuses on health conditions veterans may experience. According to VA, experts estimate that up to 20 percent of Operation Enduring Freedom and Operation Iraqi Freedom veterans have experienced post-traumatic stress disorder (PTSD) and demand for PTSD treatment is increasing. Because of the importance of research in improving the services that veterans receive, GAO was asked to report on VA's funding of PTSD research, and its processes for funding PTSD research proposals, reviewing and incorporating research outcomes into clinical practice guidelines (CPG)— tools that offer clinicians recommendations for clinical services but do not require clinicians to provide one service over another— and determining which PTSD services are required to be made available at VA facilities. To do this work, GAO obtained and summarized VA data on the funding of PTSD research from its medical and prosthetic research appropriation through its intramural research program. GAO also reviewed relevant VA documents, such as those for developing CPGs and those related to VA's 2008 *Uniform Mental Health Services in VA Medical Centers and Clinics* handbook (Handbook), which defines certain mental health services that must be made available at VA facilities. GAO also interviewed VA officials.

What GAO Found

Based on VA data GAO obtained and summarized, GAO found that the amount of funding VA provided for intramural PTSD research increased from \$9.9 million in fiscal year 2005 to \$24.5 million in fiscal year 2009. From fiscal year 2005 through fiscal year 2009, intramural PTSD research funding ranged from 2.5 percent to 4.8 percent of VA's medical and prosthetic research appropriation. In addition, the number of PTSD research studies VA funded through the Merit Review Program and the Cooperative Studies Program (CSP)—VA's two primary funding mechanisms in its intramural research program—increased from 47 in fiscal year 2005 to 96 in fiscal year 2009.

According to VA officials, intramural research proposals, including those on PTSD, are funded primarily according to scientific merit in both the Merit Review

Program and CSP. Proposals are evaluated by a panel of reviewers and scored based on their scientific merit. Directors of VA's research and development services—offices that focus on different research areas and administer VA's intramural research program—fund proposals based on their scores, typically up to a specified percentile. The number of proposals funded may vary based on budgetary considerations and, for a small number of proposals, responsiveness to VA research priority areas.

VA has a process to review and incorporate relevant research outcomes to develop CPGs for a number of topics, including PTSD. VA relies on the policies of a joint VA and Department of Defense (DOD) work group—comprised of VA and DOD officials—to ensure that systematic reviews of relevant research outcomes are conducted when issuing CPGs.

In brief, a systematic review is conducted to identify the most methodologically rigorous research studies that are applicable to each clinical question contained in the CPG. A group of subject matter experts then assesses the individual research studies in order to determine the overall quality of evidence available for each particular clinical question, considers the potential benefits and harms of a clinical intervention to determine its net effect, and, based on an assessment of the overall quality of the evidence and the net effect of an intervention, develops recommendations for the CPG.

According to VA officials, the decision to require that two PTSD services— cognitive processing therapy and prolonged exposure therapy—be made available at VA facilities by including them in the Handbook was based on a review of research outcomes and the availability of existing resources. Specifically, VA officials told GAO that these two services were strongly recommended in the 2004 PTSD CPG and had greater evidence supporting their effectiveness than other PTSD services. VA also told GAO that prior to the Handbook's 2008 issuance, VA had already begun investing resources in training programs for cognitive processing therapy in 2006 and prolonged exposure therapy in 2007.

While VA provided some documentation regarding the decision-making process for PTSD services, VA officials explained that clinical decision-making processes are not typically expected to be documented in a formal manner. VA officials told GAO that they are currently clarifying language in the Handbook but do not plan to revise any requirements relating to PTSD services at this time.

VA provided technical comments that GAO incorporated as appropriate.

January 24, 2011

The Honorable Michael H. Michaud
Ranking Member
Subcommittee on Health
Committee on Veterans' Affairs
House of Representatives

Dear Mr. Michaud:

In addition to providing health care to about 5 million veterans each year, the Department of Veterans Affairs (VA) also funds research that focuses on the specific health conditions that veterans may experience. One condition that is examined in VA-funded research is post-traumatic stress disorder (PTSD), an anxiety disorder that can occur after a person is exposed to a life-threatening event.[1] Veterans diagnosed with PTSD may experience problems sleeping, maintaining relationships, and returning to their previous civilian lives.[2] According to VA, experts estimate that up to 20 percent of Operation Enduring Freedom and Operation Iraqi Freedom veterans,[3] up to 10 percent of Gulf War veterans, and up to 30 percent of Vietnam War veterans have experienced PTSD.[4] Consequently, demand for PTSD treatment continues to grow. VA data show that from fiscal year 2004 through fiscal year 2008, the number of unique veterans receiving treatment for PTSD increased by 60 percent from over 274,000 to over 442,000. In particular, the number of Operation Iraqi Freedom and Operation Enduring Freedom veterans who received VA treatment for PTSD increased from nearly 4,400 in fiscal year 2004 to over 69,000 in fiscal year 2008.

Veterans diagnosed with PTSD can receive a range of treatments to manage their symptoms, including individual and group therapy and medication. Veterans can receive PTSD treatment on an outpatient basis at VA facilities such as medical centers, community-based outpatient clinics, and Vet Centers.[5] Veterans can also receive intensive treatment through VA medical center inpatient settings for acute care needs and through esidential rehabilitation treatment programs for more prolonged rehabilitative care.

VA has guidance and policies in place related to PTSD services. For example, in 2004, the joint VA/Department of Defense (DOD) Evidence-Based Practice Work Group[6] issued a CPG for PTSD.[7] The PTSD CPG is an educational tool for clinicians that provides evidence-based recommendations[8] for PTSD services based on a review of PTSD research outcomes. It does not require clinicians to provide one service over another. However, in a handbook issued in 2008—*Uniform Mental Health Services in VA Medical Centers and Clinics* (Handbook)—VA for the first time required certain mental health services to be made available to veterans throughout the system.[9] For PTSD, the Handbook requires that cognitive processing therapy or prolonged exposure therapy, two evidence-based psychotherapies, be provided or made available at VA facilities.[10]

Through its intramural research program, VA funds studies on different topics, such as PTSD. VA intramural studies are conducted by VA investigators—that is, researchers who conduct VA research studies. VA intramural research refers to research that is funded by and conducted within VA. In fiscal year 2009, VA received an appropriation of $510 million for medical and prosthetic research.[11] This appropriation funds VA's intramural research program, including providing funding for necessary equipment and supplies.[12] VA also receives three medical care appropriations that support VA's intramural research by paying some of the costs associated with this research, for example, the salaries of VA investigators who are also VA clinicians.[13] According to VA, in fiscal year 2009, VA's medical care appropriations totaled about $41 billion and VA provided $433 million of that amount to support all research conducted at VA facilities.[14]

Because of the growing demand for PTSD services and the importance of research in improving the health care services that veterans receive, you asked us to report on VA's funding of PTSD research, VA's processes for reviewing PTSD research proposals, VA's incorporation of research outcomes into clinical practice, and VA's process for determining which PTSD services it requires VA facilities to provide or make available. This report will describe

- how much funding VA provided for intramural PTSD research from its medical and prosthetic research appropriations from fiscal year 2005 through fiscal year 2009,
- how VA determines which intramural PTSD research studies will be funded,
- how VA reviews PTSD research outcomes and incorporates them into its PTSD CPG, and
- how VA determines which PTSD services it requires VA facilities to provide or make available.

To describe how much funding VA provided for PTSD research from its medical and prosthetic research appropriations through its intramural research program from fiscal year 2005 through fiscal year 2009, we obtained and summarized data provided by VA's Office of Research and Development (ORD), the office that manages the Merit Review Program and the Cooperative Studies Program (CSP)—the two primary funding mechanisms within VA's intramural research program.[15] VA officials define PTSD research as "the effort to acquire generalizable knowledge about causes, epidemiology, susceptibility and genetics, resilience, pathophysiology, prevention and treatment of post-traumatic stress disorder." Based on these data, for fiscal years 2005 through 2009, we calculated totals and trends for (1) overall intramural PTSD research funding—including PTSD research studies and other PTSD research-related funding, such as career development awards provided to junior VA investigators to conduct PTSD studies, salaries for VA investigators who are not VA clinicians,[16] funding for PTSD research conducted within ORD research centers, and PTSD research meetings, and (2) the number and type of intramural PTSD research studies funded. According to VA, the funding data we obtained from VA do not include funds provided to conduct or support intramural PTSD research from VA's medical care appropriations.[17] Because of this, they do not necessarily represent all the funding VA provided for PTSD research during this time. In addition, to obtain information about how VA funds research conducted at VA, we interviewed officials from VA's Veterans Health Administration's Office of Finance, ORD, and Veterans Integrated Service Networks.[18] We also reviewed VA documents regarding its total medical and prosthetic research appropriations. We tested the internal consistency and reliability of the PTSD research data by reviewing the data for obvious outliers and performing consistency checks. We found the data to be sufficiently reliable for the purposes of this report.[19]

To describe how VA determines which intramural PTSD research studies will be funded, we interviewed VA officials responsible for managing VA's intramural research program. We also obtained and analyzed VA documents that describe VA's policies for submitting, reviewing, and funding intramural research proposals. In addition, to understand the process VA uses to evaluate intramural research proposals, we observed a meeting in which research proposals were evaluated.

To describe how VA reviews PTSD research outcomes and incorporates them into its PTSD CPG to inform clinical practice at VA, we interviewed VA officials who are responsible for developing CPGs. We also obtained and reviewed the PTSD CPG and documents related to CPG development.

To describe how VA determines which PTSD services it requires VA facilities to provide or make available to veterans, we interviewed VA officials responsible for determining these requirements. We also obtained and reviewed documents that describe the PTSD service requirements.

We conducted this performance audit from May 2010 through November 2010 in accordance with generally accepted government auditing standards. Those standards require that we plan and perform the audit to obtain sufficient, appropriate evidence to provide a reasonable basis for our findings and conclusions based on our audit objectives. We believe that the evidence obtained provides a reasonable basis for our findings and conclusions based on our audit objectives.

BACKGROUND

VA manages its intramural research program through ORD. According to ORD's 2009 to 2014 strategic plan, ORD has 10 research priority areas, which are topics of research that are considered important to VA.[20] The research priority areas are the health care needs of veterans who have served in Operation Enduring Freedom and Operation Iraqi Freedom, aging-related conditions, mental health care and well-being, chronic diseases, long-term care and caregiving, deployment-related exposure to hazardous environmental agents, equity in care, access in rural areas, women's health, and personalized medicine. According to VA officials, all of these research priority areas could include PTSD research. VA funds intramural research through the following:

- VA's Merit Review Program: This program supports research studies typically conducted by one VA investigator at one VA facility and is administered by ORD's four research and development services, each of which has a different research focus. (See table 1.) Each research and development service is responsible for soliciting, reviewing, selecting, and funding research proposals submitted to the service.
- VA's CSP: This program, which is administered by Clinical Science, funds larger-scale, multisite clinical trials and epidemiological research studies on key diseases that impact veterans.

The Merit Review Program has research award funding limits, which are set by VA. In some cases, intramural research awards may only be funded for a certain number of years. See table 2 for more information.

Table 1. The Office of Research and Development's Research and Development Services

Research and development service	Focus of research	Examples of research
Biomedical Laboratory	Biological or physiological principles in humans or animals	Investigations of tissues, blood, or other biologic specimens
Clinical Science	Human beings	Clinical studies examining interventions and effectiveness; epidemiological studies
Health Services	The interface of health care systems, patients, and health care outcomes	Studies examining quality, access, patient outcomes, and costs
Rehabilitation	Improving the quality of life of impaired and disabled veterans	Veteran rehabilitation studies; studies focused on identifying technical solutions forimpaired and disabled veterans

Source: GAO analysis of Department of Veterans Affairs information.

Table 2. Department of Veterans Affairs (VA) Intramural Research Study Funding Limits and Maximum Length of Award by Research and Development Service

Service	Funding limit per award per fiscal year		Maximum length of award (in fiscal years)	
	Pilot study[a]	Full study	Pilot study[a]	Full study
Biomedical Laboratory	N/A	$150,000[b]	N/A	4
Clinical Science	N/A	$150,000[b]	N/A	4 (5 for clinical trials)
Cooperative Studies Program	N/A	No limit	N/A	No limit
Health Services	$100,000	$300,000[c]	1	4
Rehabilitation	$75,000	$300,000	2	4

Source: GAO analysis of VA information.

[a] A pilot study is a study to establish feasibility or to develop data, a technique, a concept, or a procedure, which is preliminary to undertaking a full study. Two of VA's Office of Research and Development's research and development services—Health Services and Rehabilitation—accept pilot study proposals in addition to full study proposals.

[b] According to VA officials, this limit may be exceeded for funding the salaries of investigators who are not VA clinicians or for equipment.

[c] According to VA officials, the total over all years may not exceed $925,000.

In addition to individual studies conducted at VA facilities, VA has several research centers and programs that conduct or support PTSD research. For example, the National Center for PTSD focuses on PTSD research.VA also has Research Enhancement Award Programs, which help support PTSD research by providing staff and other resources to investigators. (For more information on VA research centers and research programs that conduct or support PTSD research, see app. I.) According to a VA official from the National Center for PTSD, VA does not fund most of the PTSD research that is being conducted today.

Origin and Criteria for Intramural Research Proposals

Intramural research proposals may be service-directed—solicited by ORD on specific topics—or investigator-initiated— submitted by investigators to ORD on their own initiative.

Investigators submit proposals either in response to a request for proposals on a specific topic (for service-directed proposals) or to an open request for proposals (for investigator-initiated proposals). For both the Merit Review Program and CSP, proposals are typically evaluated in two review cycles per year.[21]

To be considered for intramural research funding:[22]

- The proposal must be veteran-centric.
- The proposal must have received approval from the director of the medical center and the research and development office of the medical center where the lead investigator, known as a principal investigator, is based.[23]
- The principal investigator and any coprincipal investigators must demonstrate a primary professional commitment to VA, as demonstrated by at least a 5/8 time VA appointment at the time the funding is awarded and previous VA experience, including experience in research and patient care.[24]
- Research must be conducted primarily on VA premises. The principal investigator and any coprincipal investigators must have designated research space within a VA medical center.[25]

PTSD RESEARCH FUNDING INCREASED FROM FISCAL YEAR 2005 THROUGH FISCAL YEAR 2009

Overall intramural PTSD research funding from VA's medical and prosthetic research appropriation increased from $9.9 million in fiscal year 2005 to $24.5 million in fiscal year 2009. The number of intramural PTSD research studies funded through the Merit Review Program and CSP increased from 47 in fiscal year 2005 to 96 in fiscal year 2009.

VA Intramural PTSD Research Funding Increased from $9.9 Million in Fiscal Year 2005 to $24.5 Million in Fiscal Year 2009

Based on the VA data we obtained and summarized, we found that overall intramural PTSD research funding from VA's medical and prosthetic research appropriation increased from about $9.9 million in fiscal year 2005 to about $24.5 million in fiscal year 2009, or by about 150 percent (see fig. 1). Overall intramural PTSD research funding included funding for specific PTSD studies as well as for other PTSD research-related funding, such as career development awards provided to junior VA investigators to conduct PTSD studies, salaries for VA investigators who are not VA clinicians,[26] funding for PTSD research conducted within ORD research centers, and PTSD research meetings. Of the $80.2 million provided for PTSD studies from fiscal year 2005 through fiscal year 2009, $51.3 million, or about 64 percent, was for studies funded through the Merit Review Program. The remaining approximately $28.9 million, or about 36 percent, was for CSP studies. (See fig. 2.) From fiscal year 2005 through fiscal year 2009, intramural PTSD research funding ranged from 2.5 percent to 4.8 percent of VA's medical and prosthetic research appropriation. (See table 3 for VA intramural PTSD research funding and VA's medical and prosthetic research appropriations from fiscal year 2005 through fiscal year 2009.) For comparison,[27] according to a 2009 report prepared by ORD staff for VA's National Research Advisory Council,[28] for fiscal year 2009, funding for intramural traumatic brain injury research was about $14.6 million, 2.9 percent of the medical and prosthetic research appropriation. Funding for spinal cord injury research was $27.2 million, 5.3 percent of the medical and prosthetic research appropriation. Funding for intramural cardiovascular disease and stroke research was $53.1 million, 10.4 percent of the medical and prosthetic research appropriation.

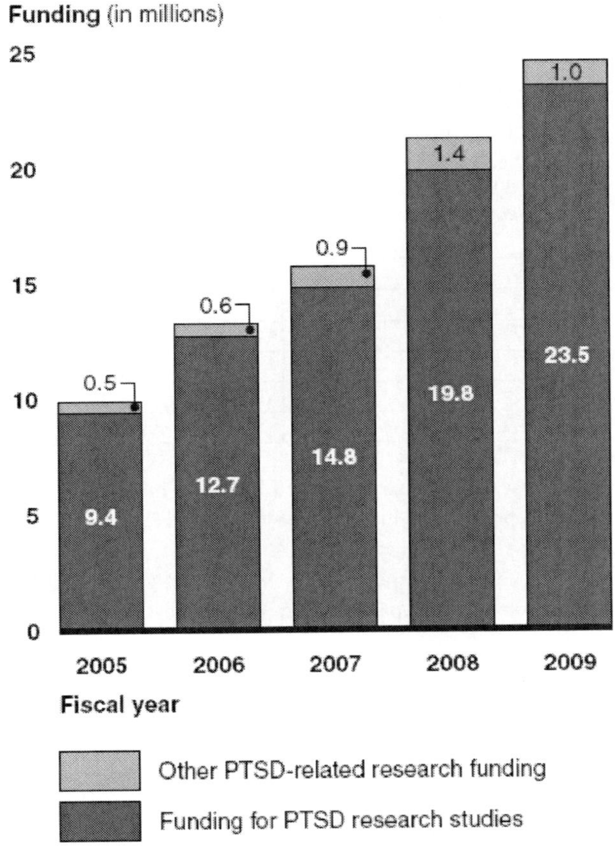

Source: GAO analysis of VA data.

Figure 1. Department of Veterans Affairs (VA) Intramural Funding for Post-Traumatic Stress Disorder (PTSD) Research Studies and Other PTSD Research-Related Funding, Fiscal Years 2005 through 2009.

The Number of PTSD Studies Funded through VA's Intramural Research Program Increased from 47 in Fiscal Year 2005 to 96 in Fiscal Year 2009

Similarly, we found that the number of PTSD studies funded from VA's medical and prosthetic research appropriations through VA's intramural research program increased from fiscal year 2005 through fiscal year 2009. (See fig. 3.)

Table 3. Department of Veterans Affairs (VA) Intramural Post-Traumatic Stress Disorder (PTSD) Research Funding and VA's Medical and Prosthetic Research Appropriation, Fiscal Years 2005 through 2009

Dollars in millions			
Fiscal year	VA intramural PTSD research funding	VA's medical and prosthetic research appropriation	Percentage
2005	$9.9	$390.2	2.5
2006	13.3	412.0	3.2
2007	15.7	446.5	3.5
2008	21.3	480.0	4.4
2009	24.5	510.0	4.8
Total	$84.7	$2,238.7	3.8

Source: GAO analysis of VA data.

Note: VA intramural research is also supported by VA's medical care appropriations, which are not represented in this table. For example, the medical care appropriations pay for the salaries of VA investigators who are VA clinicians (according to VA, about 70 percent of VA investigators are VA clinicians), administrative costs such as payroll and human resources, and logistical and infrastructure costs.

Specifically, in fiscal year 2005, 47 intramural PTSD research studies were funded while in fiscal year 2009, 96 intramural PTSD research studies were funded.[29] This represented an increase of more than 100 percent. Of all the studies funded each fiscal year, only a small number were CSP studies.

VA Intramural PTSD Research Studies Are Funded Primarily According to Scientific Merit

According to VA officials, intramural research proposals, including those on PTSD, are reviewed and funded in VA's Merit Review Program and VA's CSP primarily according to scientific merit.

VA's Merit Review Program. Intramural research proposals submitted to VA's Merit Review Program are reviewed through a series of steps prior to funding. See figure 4 for an overview of the submission, review, and funding process for proposals submitted to the Merit Review Program. (For more detailed information on this process, see app. II.)

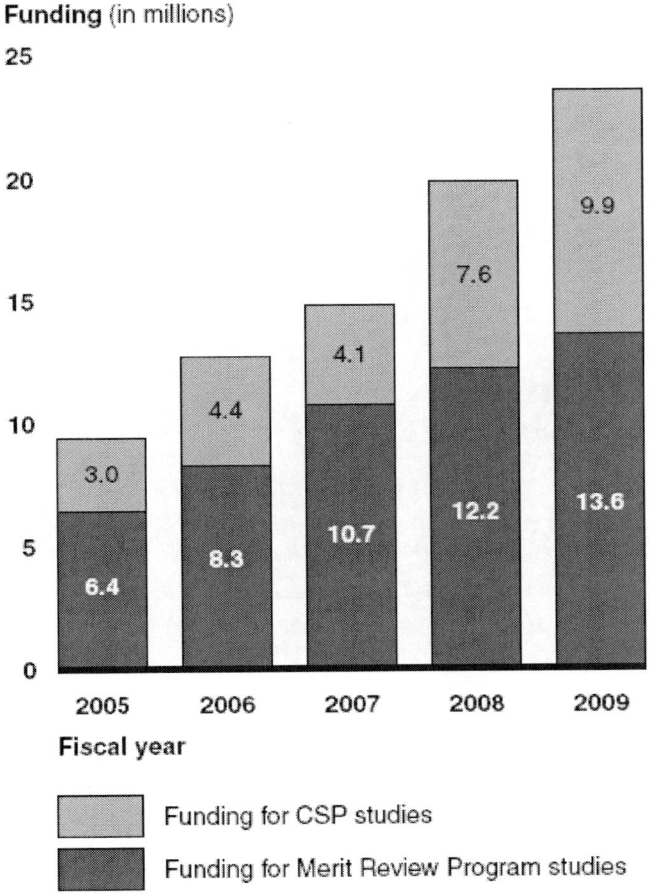

Source: GAO analysis of VA data.

Figure 2. Department of Veterans Affairs (VA) Intramural Post-Traumatic Stress Disorder (PTSD) Funding for Merit Review Program Studies and Cooperative Studies Program (CSP) Studies, Fiscal Years 2005 through 2009.

First, investigators submit proposals electronically. Investigators typically submit Merit Review Program proposals to grants.gov, the government's central grant identification and proposal portal,[30] in response to a request for proposals. Submitted proposals are then transferred to eRA Commons, an electronic system for grant administration functions, for VA processing and review.[31]

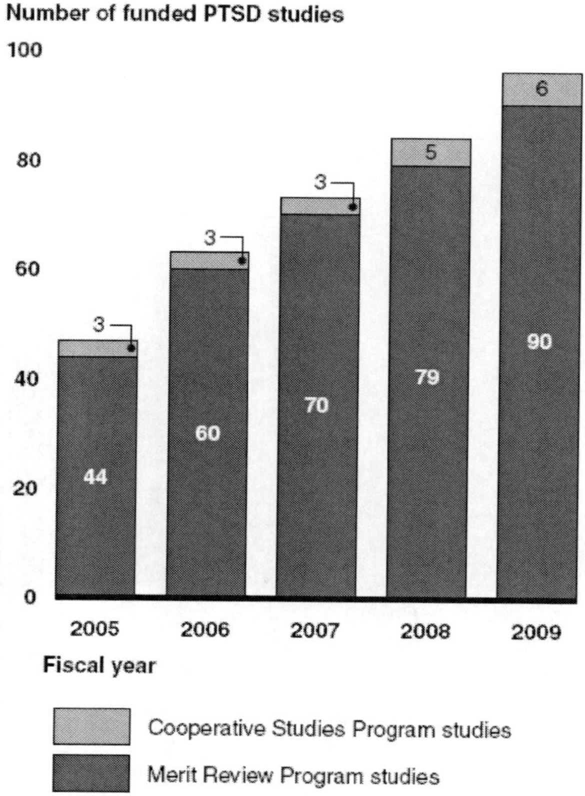

Source: GAO analysis of VA data.

Figure 3. Number of Department of Veterans Affairs (VA) Intramural Post-Traumatic Stress Disorder (PTSD) Research Studies Funded per Fiscal Year, Fiscal Years 2005 through 2009.

Second, each proposal is assigned to a merit review panel for evaluation. Each merit review panel reviews proposals in a specific research topic area, and is composed of panelists, typically associate-level professors, who are selected based on their expertise in this area.[32] According to VA documents, as of 2010, there were a total of 35 merit review panels across VA's research and development services.[33] The merit review panels evaluate each proposal based on its scientific merit.[34] Panelists consider several criteria in evaluating the overall scientific merit of a proposal. (See table 4 for criteria used to determine scientific merit.)

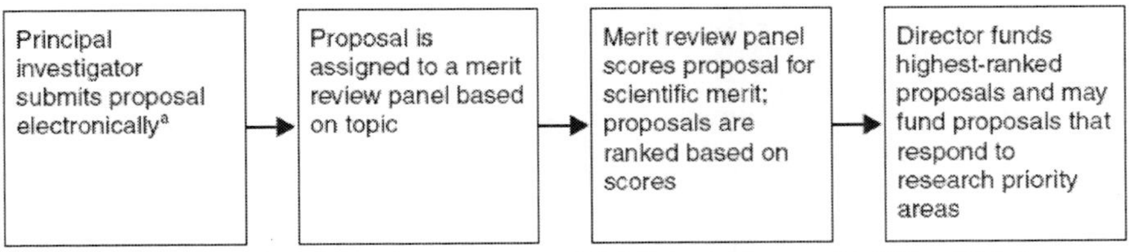

Source: GAO analysis of VA documents and GAO interviews with VA officials.

[a] Proposals are submitted electronically to grants, the government's central grant identification and proposal portal. Proposals are then transferred to eRA Commons, an electronic system for grant administration functions, for VA processing and review.

Figure 4. Overview of Submission, Review, and Funding Process in Department of Veterans Affairs' (VA) Merit Review Program.

Table 4. Scientific Merit Scoring Criteria in the Department of Veterans Affairs' (VA) Merit Review Program

Criteria	Description
Significance	Supports/advances the health and health care of veterans and research field in general; addresses important scientific question/area; makes a potential contribution to scientific literature.
Approach	Incorporates current scientific/theoretical bases; is hypothesis-driven; uses appropriate research design/methods for addressing hypothesis; ensures that feasibility of methods is clear.
Innovation	Addresses new concepts, gaps, or both, in the research area; addresses potential for impact of findings on existing field of research, treatment paradigms, or both.
Environment	Has appropriate knowledge/background and resources (e.g., equipment and staff) to ensure completion of study.
Feasibility	Provides sufficient evidence to determine that the proposed study can besuccessfully conducted and completed.
Investigator	Ensures that investigators involved in the proposed study are appropriately trained and have expertise in the proposed area of research.

Source: GAO analysis of VA information.

Third, the merit review panelists score the proposals to determine their rank. Each panelist provides a score to each of the proposals reviewed by the panel. The scores are averaged to create a "priority score" for the proposal.[35] (See app. II for specific scoring guidelines given to panelists in all research and development services.) All proposals scored by the merit review panel are then ranked by priority score among all of the proposal scores recently assigned by the merit review panel. The rank of the proposal is used to determine the "percentile" of the proposal.[36]

Finally, research and development service directors determine how many proposals to fund. All of the proposals scored by all merit review panels in a research and development service in the review cycle are ranked together by their percentiles to be considered for funding. According to VA officials, research and development service directors typically fund up to the 25th percentile of proposals in a review cycle, beginning with those with the most scientific merit, although the number of proposals funded may vary depending on the budget. According to VA, research and development service directors may also choose to fund a small number of additional proposals at the margin that respond to research priority areas. For example, if the fundable range determined by a research and development service director was up to the 25th percentile, proposals at the 26th percentile related to research priority areas could also be considered for funding.[37]

VA's Cooperative Studies Program: VA intramural research proposals submitted to CSP are reviewed and scored in a process similar to that of the Merit Review Program prior to consideration for funding. To help develop the CSP proposal, investigators are assisted by members of a CSP center,[38] a VA entity that provides guidance and support for research across multiple sites. (See fig. 5 for an overview of the process for submitting, reviewing, and funding a CSP proposal. For more information on ORD's CSP review process, see app. III.)

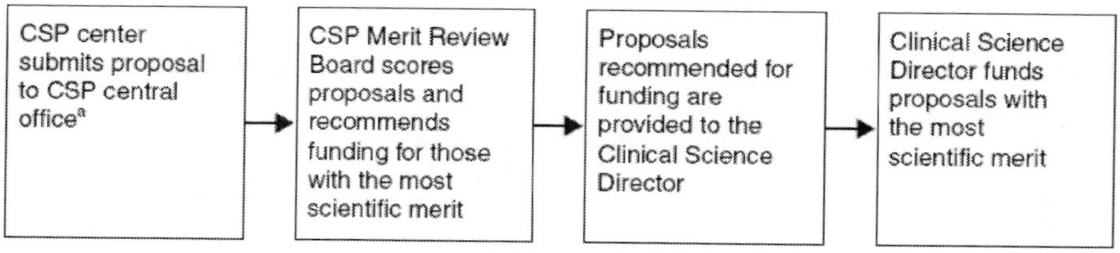

Source: GAO analysis of VA documents and GAO interviews with VA officials.

[a] Prior to submitting the proposal to CSP central office, the principal investigator must have a letter of intent approved by the Director of Clinical Science.

Figure 5. Overview of Submission, Review, and Funding for a Department of Veterans Affairs' (VA) Cooperative Studies Program (CSP) Proposal.

Before submitting a research proposal, investigators submit a letter of intent, or a preliminary outline of a proposal, to the Director of Clinical Science to be approved for planning a CSP proposal.[39] Based on the merit of the letter of intent, as determined by three or more reviewers,[40] the Clinical Science Director decides whether to fund planning efforts to develop a CSP proposal.[41] When the principal investigator receives approval to begin planning efforts, the Clinical Science Director assigns a CSP center to provide statistical and methodological guidance to the investigator. The director of the CSP center designates a project manager and methodologist, such as a person with expertise in biostatistics, to provide guidance to the principal investigator. The Clinical Science Director, with recommendations from the principal investigator, then forms a planning committee of additional experts to assist in developing a CSP proposal. The planning committee develops a CSP proposal over the course of two planning meetings.

Once a proposal is developed, the CSP center, on behalf of the principal investigator, submits a hard copy proposal to the CSP central office for evaluation by the Cooperative Studies Scientific Merit Review Board.[42] This board consists of reviewers who have extensive experience in clinical research and the conduct of clinical trials or epidemiology studies.[43] Reviewers evaluate CSP proposals based on scientific merit. According to VA, the scientific merit of a CSP proposal is defined by the importance of the proposal, its feasibility, the clarity and achievability of its objectives, the adequacy of the plan of investigation, the correctness of the technical details, and the adequacy of the safeguards for the welfare of the patients.[44] Based on these criteria, reviewers discuss the general scientific merit of the proposal. Reviewers vote on whether to unconditionally approve, conditionally approve, reject or defer with recommendation for resubmittal, or reject each proposal. (See table 5 for an overview of funding recommendations provided by the board.)

Table 5. Overview of Funding Recommendations Provided by the Department of Veterans Affairs' (VA) Cooperative Studies Scientific Merit Review Board

Recommendation for funding	Definition
Unconditional approval	The proposal is approved without changes oradditions to the proposal.
Conditional approval	The proposal is approved pending certain changes or additions to the proposal.
Rejection or defer with recommendation for resubmittal	The proposal is considered to be worthwhile, but is in need of major revisions. A revised proposal can be resubmitted to the Clinical Science Director.
Rejection	The proposal is rejected. The principal investigator must submit a new request for planning to submit a revised proposal.

Source: GAO analysis of a VA document.

After the reviewers vote, they each provide scores for a proposal recommended for funding based on scientific merit.[45] The scores are then averaged to provide a priority score for a proposal. Finally, the Clinical Science Director considers the priority scores of all the proposals in that review cycle and selects the proposals with the strongest priority scores for funding. According to VA officials, the number of proposals funded may vary depending on the budget.[46]

VA Has Established a Standardized Process to Review All Relevant PTSD Research Outcomes and Incorporate Them into a PTSD CPG

The VA/DOD Evidence-Based Practice Work Group, which is responsible for developing and updating all of VA's CPGs, has a standardized and reproducible process to review all relevant research outcomes when developing or updating all CPGs, including the PTSD CPG. To develop or update a CPG, the VA/DOD Evidence-Based Practice Work Group identifies and assigns a group of VA and DOD clinical leaders and experts who are knowledgeable in the subject area to work on the CPG.[47] Generally, the process to develop or update a CPG consists of the following steps.

- First, the assigned group of VA and DOD clinical leaders and experts identifies "clinical questions" that will be answered in the CPG. According to VA officials, clinical questions can be either broad or specific. For example, the 2004 PTSD CPG contained clinical questions regarding whether early intervention is more effective than later intervention, and whether certain interventions, such as different psychotherapies, are more effective than others.
- Second, in order to minimize bias, an external contractor conducts a systematic review of relevant research and selects and summarizes the most methodologically rigorous research studies that are applicable to each of the clinical questions.
- Third, after receiving summaries of the studies with the highest level of evidence, the VA and DOD group of clinical leaders and experts rates the research using an established grading scheme that considers
    - the level of evidence of each research study—the scope and methodological rigor of an individual study;

  - o the overall quality of evidence—the overall quality of all of the research that addresses a particular clinical question, considering the level of evidence of all the studies considered; and
  - o the net effect of an intervention—according to the collective results of the studies considered, the intervention's benefits minus the intervention's harms.
- Finally, the assigned group of VA and DOD clinical leaders and experts assigns a grade to each evidence-based recommendation based on an assessment of the overall quality of evidence and the net effect of the intervention. (See app. IV for a detailed description of the process used to develop evidence-based VA/DOD CPGs.)

The process for conducting a systematic review of research outcomes to develop or update a CPG is repeated as often as is deemed necessary by the VA/DOD Evidence-Based Practice Work Group according to its written procedures and designated time frames.[48] According to VA/DOD Evidence-Based Practice Work Group documents, routine updates to the CPGs should ideally occur approximately every 2 years. However, updates to CPGs often do not occur every 2 years, and VA officials told us that some CPGs are updated more frequently than others based on availability of resources and priority areas. Additionally, VA officials reported that a CPG will be immediately updated if any evidence-based recommendation contained in it is identified as harmful to patients.

According to VA, the VA/DOD Evidence-Based Practice Work Group approved an update to the 2004 PTSD CPG on October 25, 2010, and published the update on VA's Web site on November 17, 2010.[49] According to VA officials, the systematic process outlined above was used to review all relevant research outcomes and make evidence-based recommendations for PTSD services to both develop and update the PTSD CPG.

VA Reviewed Research Outcomes and Used Existing Resources in Determining Which PTSD Services to Require Its Facilities to Provide or Make Available to Veterans

According to VA officials, the decision to require that cognitive processing therapy and prolonged exposure therapy be made available to veterans diagnosed with PTSD at VA facilities—as indicated in the Handbook, which established certain requirements for mental health services within VA—was based on a review of research outcomes and the availability of existing resources.

- *Review of research outcomes.* According to VA, agency officials and qualified subject matter experts reviewed relevant research outcomes and the quality of the research to determine the most efficacious PTSD treatments available when determining which PTSD services to include in the Handbook and make available to veterans. Specifically, VA officials told us that their decision to include cognitive processing therapy and prolonged exposure therapy in the Handbook was influenced by the fact that both of these had been graded as level "A" treatments in the 2004 PTSD CPG (indicating that the intervention is always indicated and acceptable).[50] Furthermore, VA officials said that these two therapies had greater evidence supporting their effectiveness than other PTSD services also graded as level "A" in the 2004 PTSD CPG.[51] In addition, VA officials added that their decision was validated by the results of a VA-commissioned Institute of Medicine study published in 2008 that reviewed the evidence for existing PTSD treatments. According to VA, the study found that cognitive processing therapy and prolonged exposure therapy were considered efficacious treatments for PTSD.[52] While the Institute of Medicine report was released after VA had already decided to include cognitive processing therapy and prolonged exposure therapy in the Handbook, VA officials explained that the Institute of Medicine report was the basis for the decision not to include other PTSD services in the Handbook.
- *Availability of existing resources.* VA officials told us that prior to issuing the Handbook in 2008, VA had already begun investing considerable resources to implement national training programs for cognitive processing therapy and prolonged exposure therapy in 2006 and 2007, respectively. VA officials said that they decided to implement the national training programs because VA realized the need to create sufficient capacity so that evidence-based PTSD treatments could be available to veterans throughout the VA system. VA explained that the national training programs were rolled out in advance of the Handbook's issuance as part of the implementation of VA's *Comprehensive Veterans Health Administration Strategic Plan*

> *for Mental Health Services*, which called for rapid implementation of evidence-based treatments. VA did this to ensure that it had the capacity to provide cognitive processing therapy and prolonged exposure therapy to all veterans with PTSD for whom these treatments were clinically appropriate.[53] VA officials said that they were able to begin implementing national training programs for cognitive processing therapy in 2006 and prolonged exposure therapy in 2007 because VA had qualified instructors to administer the programs and money available to fund them.[54]

Unlike the written and standardized process that the VA/DOD Evidence-Based Practice Work Group established to develop CPGs, VA does not have a formal written process or framework to explain its decision for including cognitive processing therapy and prolonged exposure therapy in the Handbook.[55]

VA officials explained that they followed a process when choosing cognitive processing therapy and prolonged exposure therapy, but added that clinical decision-making processes are not typically expected to be documented in a formal manner.

VA officials told us that they plan to assess the implementation of the Handbook and will update PTSD requirements in it as needed or as new information or unexpected obstacles arise in the future.[56] VA officials stated that they are currently clarifying the language regarding some of the requirements, but do not plan to revise any of the requirements relating to PTSD services at this time.

AGENCY COMMENTS

We provided a draft of this report to VA and received technical comments, which we incorporated into our report as appropriate.

Sincerely yours,
Randall B. Williamson Director, Health Care
Enclosures – V

APPENDIX I: VA RESEARCH CENTERS AND PROGRAMS THAT CONDUCT OR SUPPORT PTSD RESEARCH

In addition to post-traumatic stress disorder (PTSD) research studies that are conducted by individual Department of Veterans Affairs (VA) investigators, or researchers, VA also funds a number of research centers or programs that conduct or support PTSD research. See table 6 for a description of these VA research centers and programs.

Table 6. Department of Veterans Affairs (VA) Research Centers and Programs That Conduct or Support Post-Traumatic Stress Disorder (PTSD) Research

VA research centers/programs	Description	Established by Congress?	Number of centers or programs with a primary focus on PTSD
Office of Mental Health Services			
The National Center for PTSD	Advances the clinical care and social welfare of veterans through research, education, and training in the science, diagnosis, and treatment of PTSD and stress-related disorders.	Yes	1[a]
Centers of Excellence	Research the causes and treatments of mental disorders and use the dissemination of education to implement new knowledge into routine VA clinical practices.	Yes	2
Mental Illness Research, Education, and Clinical Centers	Research the causes and treatments of mental disorders and use education to implement knowledge into routine clinical practice in VA.	Yes	4
Office of Research and Development			
Centers of Excellence	Create or maintain a core program of investigators to support and facilitate the development of research studies and train and mentor new investigators.	No	8

VA research centers/programs	Description	Established by Congress?	Number of centers or programs with a primary focus on PTSD
Quality Enhancement Research Initiative Program	Enhances the quality and outcomes of VA health care by implementing research findings and evidence-based recommendations into routine clinical practice.	No	1[b]
Research Enhancement Award Programs	Support groups of VA investigators that address specific medical problems of veterans to promote innovative research, train new medical research investigators, and foster new research collaborations among investigators.	No	1

Source: GAO analysis of VA information.

[a]The National Center for PTSD, headquartered in White River Junction, Vermont, has seven divisions in five locations across the country.

[b] Although the Mental Health Quality Enhancement Research Initiative (one of nine Quality Enhancement Research Initiative Centers) focuses on depression and schizophrenia, Office of Research and Development officials stated that within the past few years it has become more involved with PTSD research.

APPENDIX II: THE REVIEW PROCESS FOR VA'S MERIT REVIEW PROGRAM

Research proposals submitted to the Department of Veterans Affairs' (VA) Merit Review Program are evaluated in merit review panels that each review proposals in a specific research topic area.

Each merit review panel is comprised of panelists, typically associate-level professors, who are selected based on their expertise in the area. Panelists are responsible for scoring proposals based on scientific merit to provide funding recommendations.

See figure 6 for a detailed description of the Merit Review Program's process for reviewing research proposals and table 7 for the Merit Review Program's scoring guidelines.

1. The portfolio manager, an official responsible for managing a specific area of research, assigns three panelists as the primary, secondary, and tertiary panelists for each research proposal. These panelists are responsible for reviewing the proposal prior to the panel meeting, and individually submitting a preliminary score and summary of the proposal into eRA Commons, an electronic system for grant administration functions, for VA processing and review. The preliminary scores range from 1.0 and 5.0 (with scores closer to 1.0 being more meritorious).

↓

2. The primary, secondary, and tertiary panelists present their preliminary scores to the entire panel[a] and respond to feedback provided by the other panelists about the proposal.[b]

↓

3. Based on the discussion at the panel meeting, the primary, secondary, and tertiary panelists can change their preliminary scores. The primary, secondary, and tertiary panelists must announce to the panel the final score each plans to give the proposal. The final scores also range from 1.0 and 5.0 (with scores closer to 1.0 being more meritorious).

↓

4. The portfolio manager asks if any panelist plans to score the research proposal 0.3 points above or below the range of the final scores provided by the primary, secondary, and tertiary panelists. If any panelist intends to score outside of this range, the panelist must discuss this decision with the rest of the panel and explain reasons for doing so.

↓

5. All panelists on the review panel then submit a final score for the research proposal. The average of the final scores multiplied by 100 is known as the priority score. In addition, the primary panelist writes a summary of the discussion of the panel meeting and submits the summary into eRA Commons.

Source: GAO analysis of VA documents and GAO interviews with VA officials.

[a] According to VA's policy, panelists who have a conflict of interest with a given proposal are required to leave the meeting before the proposal is discussed and do not score the proposal. According to VA, a conflict of interest exists when a reviewer has an interest in a research proposal that is likely to bias his or her evaluation of it. Panelists are expected to inform the portfolio manager if they have a conflict of interest.

[b] In some instances, research proposals are streamlined, meaning that they are evaluated only by the primary, secondary, and tertiary panelists, and are not discussed by the entire merit review panel. Proposals may be streamlined if the average of the primary, secondary, and tertiary panelists' preliminary scores falls in the upper half of the range of scores, indicating less merit. According to VA officials, proposals with a preliminary score of lower than 2.2, indicating very good or excellent, are also streamlined for two research and development services. (See table 7 for merit review process scoring guidelines.) In these instances, the administrator of the merit review panel meeting asks the panelists if anyone has an objection to streamlining the proposal. If a panelist objects, the proposal is discussed in the merit review panel meeting and it is not streamlined. Streamlined proposals with preliminary scores that fall in the upper half of the range of scores, indicating less merit, are not considered for funding.

Figure 6. Summary of the Department of Veterans Affairs' (VA) Merit Review Process for the Merit Review Program.

Table 7. Scoring Guidelines for the Department of Veterans Affairs' (VA) Merit Review Program

Scoring range and grade	Description
1.0 – 1.5 Excellent	Proposed research addresses important scientific area that lacks needed knowledge. Hypothesis(es)is clearly stated and research design/methodology is appropriate. Research is innovative, representing state-of-the-art science. Potential findings may have a vital role in advancing the health and health care of veterans and research in general. Resources listed suggest a very high probabilityof the study's completion.
1.6 – 2.2 Very good	Proposed research addresses important scientific area. Hypothesis(es) is clearly stated and the research design/methodology is appropriate with a few minor exceptions. Potential findings may have an important role to the health and health care of veterans and research in general. Resources listed suggest a high probability of the study's completion.
2.3 – 2.8 Good	Proposed research addresses a valid area of investigation. Hypothesis(es) is clearly stated, but research design/methodology contains key flaws that should be corrected. Potential findings may contribute to the health and health care of veterans and research in general. Resources listed suggest that the study could be completed.
2.9 – 3.4 Fair	Proposed research requires further preliminary data to warrant investigation as a viable area of research. Hypothesis(es) is not clear, research design/methods contain significant flaws, or both. It isnot clear how potential findings would contribute to the health and health care of veterans and research in general. It is unclear whether the resources listed are sufficient to ensure study completion.
3.5 – 5.0 Poor	Proposed research does not appear to address an important scientific question/area. Hypothesis(es) is not clearly stated, research design/methodology is inappropriate or contains uncorrectable flaws, or both. Design/methodological limitations hinder any significant conclusions that would contribute to the health and health care of veterans, research in general, or both. Resources listed do not suggest that the study will be completed.

Source: GAO analysis of VA documents.

Appendix III: The Review Process for VA's Cooperive Studies Program

Research proposals submitted to the Department of Veterans Affairs' (VA) Cooperative Studies Program (CSP) are reviewed and scored by the Cooperative Studies Scientific Merit Review Board. Reviewers on the board are chosen based on their expertise in clinical or epidemiological research. They typically serve 4-year terms, and ad hoc members can be added depending on specific expertise that may be needed to review a proposal. According to VA, as of October 2010, there were six reviewers on the board.

During the research proposal review process, the study team—which includes the lead researcher (referred to as the principal investigator) and a methodologist, such as a person with expertise in biostatistics—has an interactive discussion with the board regarding the proposal.[1] Reviewers evaluate CSP proposals based on scientific merit and provide scores to reflect their funding recommendations. See figure 7 for a detailed description of the review process for CSP research proposals.

1. The Deputy Director of CSP assigns three individuals on the Cooperative Studies Scientific Merit Review Board to be the initial reviewers for a CSP proposal. One of the initial reviewers is designated as the primary reviewer. All three initial reviewers prepare written reviews of the proposal based on scientific merit prior to the board meeting.[a]

↓

2. A first board meeting is held to summarize and discuss the key critiques of the written reviews provided by the initial reviewers. The primary reviewer is responsible for introducing the proposal to the board. The study team, which includes the principal investigator and a methodologist, such as a person with expertise in biostatistics, is not present at this meeting.

↓

3. A second board meeting is held with the study team.[b] At the beginning of this meeting, the principal investigator is provided a summary of the critiques discussed in the first board meeting. The study team is then given 15 minutes to provide a summary of the proposal, including its importance to VA, and to address the critiques.[c]

↓

4. After the study team responds to the board, the board and the study team engage in an interactive discussion regarding the proposal.

↓

5. After the interactive discussion, the study team is dismissed and the board votes on whether to unconditionally approve, conditionally approve, reject or defer with recommendation for resubmittal, or reject funding of the proposal.[d] For proposals that are conditionally and unconditionally approved, each member of the board assigns a numeric rating from 10 to 50, with lower scores indicating more meritorious proposals, based on scientific merit. The average of the scores for each proposal is considered the priority score.[e]

Source: GAO analysis of VA documents and GAO interviews with VA officials.

[a] According to a VA document, the primary reviewers are typically a biostatistician and a clinician. Reviewers are asked to comment on the importance of the proposal, its feasibility, the clarity and achievability of its objectives, the adequacy of the plan of investigation, the correctness of the technical details, the adequacy of the safeguards for the welfare of the patients, and any other pertinent features of the proposal. According to VA, these criteria are components of scientific merit.

[b] For CSP proposals that involve economic analysis, a health economist is also present at the board meeting to discuss the proposal. In addition, the principal investigator may ask the Clinical Science Director to allow consultants to be present at the board meeting if review of the proposal requires expertise in a specific area.

[c] According to VA, if there are any economic issues raised relating to the proposal, the study team will be given an additional 5 minutes to address these issues with a health economist.

[d] According to a VA document, unconditional approval means a proposal is approved by the board without changes and is recommended for funding. Conditional approval means that the proposal is approved by the board pending certain changes or additions to the proposal. Reject or defer with recommendation for resubmittal means the board considers the proposal to be worthwhile, but it is need of major revisions. In this case, if the principal investigator chooses to submit a revised proposal, the Clinical Science Director may waive the requirement to submit a letter of intent. If the board rejects the proposal, the principal investigator must submit a new letter of intent to resubmit a revised proposal.

[e] After the board scores the proposal, a human rights committee typically provides a general assessment of the protection of patients' rights and welfare as described in the proposal. For studies with unique ethical considerations, this review may occur prior to the review by the Cooperative Studies Scientific Merit Review Board.

Figure 7. Summary of the Department of Veterans Affairs' (VA) Cooperative Studies Program (CSP) Review Process.

APPENDIX IV: THE GID PROCESS FOR DEVELOPING VA/DOD EVIDENCE-BASED CLINICAL PRACTICE GUIDELINES

In 1999, the Department of Veterans Affairs (VA) and the Department of Defense (DOD) formed the VA/DOD Evidence-Based Practice Work Group to issue joint VA/DOD clinical practice guidelines (CPG)—tools that provide guidance and evidence-based recommendations to clinicians regarding the most effective interventions and services for a variety of health care topics.[1] To develop or update a CPG, the VA/DOD Evidence-Based Practice Work Group has a standardized process to ensure that systematic reviews of relevant research outcomes are conducted in order to formulate evidence-based recommendations for prevention, assessment, and treatment services.

To develop or update a CPG, the VA/DOD Evidence-Based Practice Work Group identifies two clinical leaders—one from VA and one from DOD— who then help identify not more than 15 to 20 other experts in the subject area to form a "guideline working group."[2] A member of the VA/DOD Evidence-Based Practice Work Group is also selected to be an evidence chaperone for each CPG to ensure that conformity to prevailing standards for conducting high-quality systematic reviews is upheld.[3]

To determine the scope of the CPG, the guideline working group, the evidence chaperone, and a facilitator are responsible for identifying clinical questions that are to be answered by a systematic review of relevant research outcomes.[4]

According to VA officials, clinical questions can be both broad and specific. For example, the 2004 post-traumatic stress disorder CPG contained clinical questions regarding whether early intervention is more effective than later intervention and whether certain interventions, such as different psychotherapies, are more effective than others.[5]

According to VA, in order to answer these clinical questions, an external evidence center—an entity that conducts systematic reviews of research on a variety of topics—is contracted to collect and review all relevant research (including, but not limited to, VA- and DOD-sponsored research) to assess its applicability to each clinical question under consideration using explicit and reproducible methods.[6]

The evidence center then focuses its review on the best available research, that is, high-quality, methodologically rigorous studies that address health issues that impact VA and DOD populations and consider the effectiveness as well as the harms and benefits of the intervention at issue. According to VA officials, the evidence center provides summaries of only the best available research to the guideline working group for review.[7]

After receiving the summaries, the guideline working group reviews the research in sequential steps using an established rating scheme developed by the U.S. Preventive Services Task Force to formulate evidence-based recommendations.[8] See figure 8 for an overview of the steps that the guideline working group uses to formulate evidence-based recommendations.

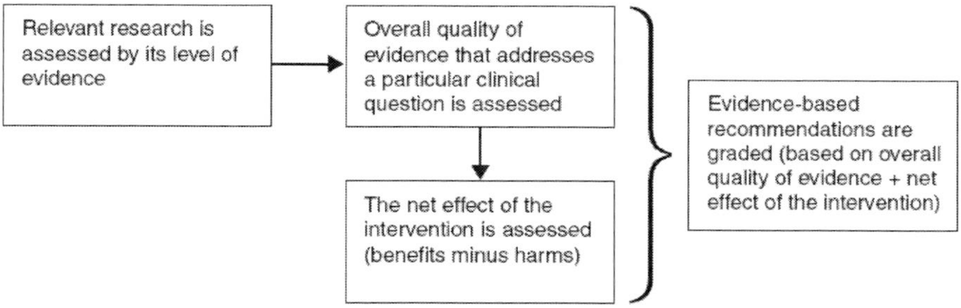

Source: GAO analysis of VA/DOD documents and GAO interviews with VA officials.

Figure 8. Overview of the Process Used by the Guideline Working Group Established by the Department of Veterans Affairs (VA)/Department of Defense (DOD) Evidence-Based Practice Work Group to Grade Evidence-Based Recommendations for Clinical Practice Guidelines.

Level of evidence. First, the guideline working group reviews the summaries to identify the level of evidence, or the level of methodological rigor. For example, research studies that have the highest quality are categorized as "I" (indicating at least one properly done randomized controlled trial), while research studies of the lowest quality are categorized as "III" (indicating that the research reflects the opinion of respected authorities, descriptive studies, case reports, and expert committees). (See table 8.)

Table 8. Categorization of Ratings Used by the Guideline Working Group Established by the Department of Veterans Affairs (VA)/Department of Defense (DOD) Evidence-Based Practice Work Group to Identify the Level of Evidence of Research Outcomes

Rating	Description
I	At least one properly done randomized controlled trial
II-1	Well-designed controlled trial without randomization
II-2	Well-designed cohort or case-control analytic study, preferably from more thanone source
II-3	Multiple time series evidence with/without intervention, dramatic results of uncontrolled experiment
III	Opinion of respected authorities, descriptive studies, case reports, and expert committees

Source: VA/DOD document.

Overall quality of research. After determining the level of evidence of individual research studies, the guideline working group makes a determination regarding the overall quality of all of the research that addresses a particular clinical question.

The overall quality takes into account the number, quality, and size of all of the individual research studies together as well as the consistency of the results between research outcomes to determine the collective overall strength of the research.

Based on this review, the guideline working group determines the overall quality of the evidence to be good, fair, or poor.[9] (See table 9.)

Table 9. Categorization of Ratings Used by the Guideline Working Group Established by the Department of Veterans Affairs (VA)/Department of Defense (DOD) Evidence-Based Practice Work Group to Determine the Overall Quality of Research

Rating	Description
Good	High-grade evidence (I or II-1) linked to health outcome
Fair	High-grade evidence (I-or II-1) linked to intermediate outcome Or Moderate-grade evidence (II-2 or II-3) directly linked to health outcome
Poor	Level III evidence or no linkage of evidence to health outcome

Source: VA/DOD document.

Net effect of the intervention. For interventions that were supported by studies of "fair" or "good" overall quality, the guideline working group evaluates the benefits and the potential harms to determine the net effect of the intervention.[10]

The net effect of an intervention takes into account the benefits of the intervention minus the harms to determine the overall potential clinical benefit that the intervention may provide to patients. The net effect of the intervention ranges from "substantial" (meaning the benefit substantially outweighs the harm) to "zero or negative" (meaning it has no impact or a negative impact on patients). (See table 10.)

Table 10. Categorization of Ratings Used by the Guideline Working Group Established by the Department of Veterans Affairs (VA)/Department of Defense (DOD) Evidence-Based Practice Work Group to Determine the Net Effect of the Intervention as Described in the Research

Rating	Description
Substantial	More than a small relative impact on a frequent condition with a substantial burden of suffering Or A large impact on an infrequent condition with a significant impact on the individual patient level
Moderate	A small relative impact on a frequent condition with a substantial burden of suffering Or A moderate impact on an infrequent condition with a significant impact on the individual patient level
Small	A negligible relative impact on a frequent condition with a substantial burden of suffering Or A small impact on an infrequent condition with a significant impact on the individual patient level
Zero or negative	Negative impact on patients Or No relative impact on either a frequent condition with a substantial burden of suffering or an infrequentcondition with a significant impact on the individual patient level

Source: VA/DOD document.

Grade of evidence-based recommendation. In the final step, the guideline working group uses its assessment of the overall quality of the evidence and the net effect of the intervention to grade evidence-based recommendations. (See table 11.)

Table 11. Grade of Evidence-Based Recommendation Assigned by the Guideline Working Group Established by the Department of Veterans Affairs (VA)/Department of Defense (DOD) Evidence-Based Practice Work Group Based on the Overall Quality of Evidence and the Net Effect of the Intervention as Described in the Research

	The net benefit of the intervention			
Overall quality of evidence	Substantial	Moderate	Small	Zero or negative
Good	A	B	C	D
Fair	B	B	C	D
Poor	I	I	I	I
Grade of recommendation	Description of recommendation			
A	A strong recommendation that the intervention is always indicated and acceptable			

Table 11. (Continued)

	The net benefit of the intervention
B	A recommendation that the intervention may be useful/effective
C	A recommendation that the intervention may be considered
D	A recommendation that a procedure may be considered not useful/effective or may be harmful
I	Insufficient evidence to recommend for or against—the clinician will use clinical judgment

Source: VA/DOD document.

End Notes

[1] American Psychiatric Association, Diagnostic and Statistical Manual of Mental Disorders, Fourth Edition, Text Revision (Washington, D.C., 2000).

[2] Those diagnosed with PTSD may also suffer from other ailments, such as depression and substance abuse.

[3] Operation Enduring Freedom, which began in October 2001, supports combat operations in Afghanistan and other locations, and Operation Iraqi Freedom, which began in March 2003, supports combat operations in Iraq and other locations. In September 2010, Operation Iraqi Freedom became known as Operation New Dawn.

[4] Estimates for veterans who have experienced PTSD vary. For example, according to VA, regarding Operation Enduring Freedom and Operation Iraqi Freedom veterans, one 2008 RAND study found that approximately 14 percent of these veterans have experienced PTSD, while another 2004 study by Hoge et al. estimated that from 6 to 20 percent of those veterans have experienced PTSD.

[5] Vet Centers offer readjustment counseling—a wide range of psychosocial services that includes individual and group counseling and screening and referrals for medical issues— to eligible veterans and their families.

[6] Formed in 1999 and composed of VA and DOD officials, the VA/DOD Evidence-Based Practice Work Group makes decisions about which clinical practice guidelines (CPG) for specific conditions will be developed and oversees their development. As of August 2010, the VA/DOD Evidence-Based Practice Work Group had issued 24 CPGs on conditions such as chronic heart failure and major depressive disorder. Since VA and DOD issue the CPGs in a joint effort, they are intended to be used by both VA and DOD clinicians. The VA/DOD Evidence-Based Practice Work Group is supported by VA's Office of Quality and Performance and the U.S. Army Medical Department's Office of Quality Management.

[7] The PTSD CPG is formally known as the VA/DOD Clinical Practice Guideline for the Management of Post-Traumatic Stress (January 2004).

[8] Evidence-based care refers to approaches that have consistently been shown in controlled research to be effective for a particular condition or conditions.

[9] Veterans Health Administration Handbook 1160.01, Uniform Mental Health Services in VA Medical Centers and Clinics (Sept. 11, 2008). According to the Handbook, all veterans with PTSD must have access to cognitive processing therapy or prolonged exposure therapy. VA medical centers and very large community-based outpatient clinics (serving more than

10,000 unique veterans each year) must be able to provide staff to administer such services at the facilities. Large (serving 5,000 to 10,000 unique veterans each year) and midsized (serving 1,500 to 5,000 unique veterans each year) community-based outpatient clinics may provide these services through telemental health or contract care when necessary. In March 2010, VA issued the Veterans Health Administration Handbook 1160.03, Programs for Veterans with Post-Traumatic Stress Disorder (PTSD), to provide additional information regarding the implementation of the PTSD requirements contained in the 2008 Handbook.

[10] Psychotherapies focus on changing individuals' behaviors, thoughts, perceptions, and emotions. Cognitive processing therapy utilizes trauma-specific cognitive techniques to help patients move past trauma-related thoughts and progress toward recovery. Prolonged exposure therapy works by helping individuals approach trauma-related thoughts, feelings, and situations that they have been avoiding because of the distress they cause. Repeated exposure to these thoughts, feelings, and situations can assist with reducing the likelihood they will cause distress.

[11] VA's medical and prosthetic research appropriation pays for necessary expenses in carrying out programs of medical and prosthetic research and development as authorized by chapter 73 of title 38, United States Code, the authorizing laws for the Veterans Health Administration. See Pub. L. No. 110-329, 122 Stat. 3574, 3706 (2008).

[12] The medical and prosthetic research appropriation funds research on different topics. It is not limited to funding research on PTSD.

[13] VA's three medical care appropriations are (1) medical services, which provides funds for the provision of veterans' health care services; (2) medical support and compliance, which provides funds for expenses related to the administration of veterans' health care services; and (3) medical facilities, which provides funds for the operation and maintenance of VA's health care facilities. Each of these appropriations provides support to all research conducted at VA facilities. For example, the medical care appropriations pay for the salaries of VA investigators who are VA clinicians (according to VA, about 70 percent of VA investigators are VA clinicians), administrative costs such as those for payroll and human resources, and logistical and infrastructure costs.

[14] VA could not provide an estimate for the amount of funding VA spent from the medical care appropriations for intramural PTSD research. Of the $433 million, more than half went to personnel costs, including the salaries of clinicians and other VA facility staff.

[15] The data provided by ORD reflect the funding amounts VA investigators were authorized to use, not necessarily the amounts that were spent. VA officials said that the authorized amounts are very similar to the amounts that are spent.

[16] Salaries for VA investigators who are VA clinicians are paid from the medical services appropriation, one of the medical care appropriations.

[17] For example, VA's Veterans Integrated Service Networks, which receive funding from the medical care appropriations and include VA's medical facilities, may also fund research by VA investigators, but this research funding is not considered part of VA's intramural research program. According to ORD officials, about 95 percent of the PTSD research funded by VA is funded by VA's intramural research program.

[18] The management of VA's medical facilities is decentralized to 21 regional networks referred to as Veterans Integrated Service Networks.

[19] In 2010, the VA Office of Inspector General found issues with ORD's validation of some research expenditure data reported by investigators at the VA Maryland Health Care System facility. See Department of Veterans Affairs, Office of Inspector General, Health Care Inspection: Inappropriate Research and Development Data Entries Affecting Veterans

Equitable Research Allocation (VERA) Funding VA Maryland Health Care System Baltimore, MD (Washington, D.C., Sept. 23, 2010). According to VA officials, the PTSD research funding data we obtained for this report were generated from a different data system than the data systems specifically examined by the VA Office of Inspector General. In addition, the PTSD research funding data are entered by VA officials at the central office and checked for accuracy by VA officials at both the central office and the facilities.

[20] In 2009, VA's Office of Inspector General found that appropriated funds for VA research addressed the broad spectrum of medical issues with which veterans contend. See Department of Veterans Affairs, Office of Inspector General, Healthcare Inspection: Review of the Veterans Health Administration's Use of Appropriated Funds for Research (Washington, D.C., 2009).

[21] According to VA, proposals may be reviewed outside of a review cycle depending on when ORD solicits requests for proposals. In rare cases, service-directed proposals are reviewed by ad hoc reviewers or solely by research and development service directors.

[22] Each research and development service may have additional requirements.

[23] The approval indicates that the medical center has agreed to commit the resources, such as space and staff, necessary to conduct the research study.

[24] Investigators who do not demonstrate a primary professional commitment to VA can request a waiver of this requirement. According to a VA document, a waiver may be granted by VA officials depending on the circumstances of the request, such as for a retired investigator who previously received funding through the Merit Review Program. According to VA, waivers are granted for about 35 investigators per year.

[25] The principal investigator and any coprincipal investigators may also have a designated research space in an approved non-VA facility or other VA facility, such as a community-based outpatient clinic.

[26] Salaries for VA investigators who are VA clinicians are paid from the medical services appropriation, one of the medical care appropriations.

[27] Because of potential overlap in research areas, percentage estimates should not be added.

[28] The National Research Advisory Council is responsible for advising the Secretary of Veterans Affairs and the Under Secretary for Health on matters related to VA's research. The Office of Management and Budget requires that the National Research Advisory Council conduct an annual assessment of VA's intramural research program.

[29] VA intramural research studies may be funded for multiple years (see table 2). Therefore, the same intramural PTSD research study funded in one fiscal year may also be funded the following fiscal year. In our analysis, this study would be counted as a funded study each fiscal year. In addition, some studies were not funded each fiscal year of their duration. For example, a study that was conducted from fiscal year 2006 through fiscal year 2009 may not have received funding in fiscal year 2007.

[30] Depending on the specific requirements of the request for proposal, a letter of intent (a preliminary outline of a research proposal) may be required prior to the submission of a research proposal.

[31] Electronic research administration, or eRA Commons, is managed and supported by the National Institutes of Health to provide support for the funding of research proposals.

[32] Merit review panelists may or may not be employed by VA. According to VA officials, most merit review panelists have previous experience reviewing proposals. According to a VA document, the number of panelists on a merit review panel may vary. For example, the number of panelists on Rehabilitation's merit review panels ranges from 16 to 59.

[33] Biomedical Laboratory and Clinical Science share the same merit review panels.

[34] In addition, for Health Services, along with scientific merit, reviewers take into account research priority areas of Health Services when scoring proposals.

[35] For Health Services, prior to assigning a priority score for a proposal, merit review panelists vote on whether to approve, conditionally approve, or reject the proposal. Conditional approval means the proposal is approved pending additions or changes. Only approved and conditionally approved proposals are assigned a priority score.

[36] According to VA, the percentile is calculated by the proposal's rank, determined by its priority score in comparison to the scores of the current and previous three review cycles, minus 0.5, divided by the total number of applications being considered. For example, if a proposal received the fifth best priority score and there were a total of 60 proposals reviewed over the four cycles, the percentile for that application would be 5 minus 0.5 divided by 60, equaling .075.

[37] After a proposal is approved for funding by the research and development service director, the proposal must undergo review by an institutional review board, an independent committee that reviews research based on ethical considerations. In addition, depending on the topic of the proposal, it may be reviewed by additional committees at this time, such as a data monitoring committee.

[38] There are nine CSP centers: VA operates five CSP Coordinating Centers to support multisite clinical trials and four Epidemiological Research and Information Centers to support epidemiology studies. In addition to receiving support from a designated CSP center, CSP proposals that involve drugs or medical devices also receive assistance from the CSP Clinical Research Pharmacy Coordinating Center, and CSP proposals that involve economic analysis receive support from VA's Health Economics Resource Center.

[39] A letter of intent typically contains an outline of the proposed research study, including justification for multiple sites where the research will be conducted and a list of experts who can assist in the initial planning efforts of the research study.

[40] Reviewers of letters of intent are selected based on their expertise in areas related to the topic of the letter of intent.

[41] Planning efforts include travel funds for personnel involved in developing the proposal. According to VA, there are two planning meetings that involve approximately 15 people.

[42] CSP proposals are currently not submitted electronically; however, ORD officials estimate that electronic submission of CSP proposals through eRA Commons will begin in fall 2011.

[43] According to a VA document, members of the Cooperative Studies Scientific Merit Review Board serve 4-year terms, and ad hoc members can be added depending on specific expertise that may be needed to review a proposal. As of October 2010, there were six members of the Cooperative Studies Scientific Merit Review Board.

[44] CSP proposals are also reviewed by a human rights committee at the designated CSP center to determine if the protection of patients' rights and welfare is adequate. CSP proposals must be approved by a human rights committee prior to being funded.

[45] Scores are given only to conditionally and unconditionally approved proposals.

[46] After a CSP proposal has received approval for funding, the proposal must undergo additional steps before study subjects are enrolled. For example, the proposal must be reviewed by an institutional review board, and an executive committee meets to review the operational and monitoring aspects of the study.

[47] In addition, representatives from VA's Office of Patient Care Services are responsible for identifying VA and DOD clinical leaders.

[48] According to VA, the development or update of a CPG typically takes 18 months.

[49] According to VA, the update of the PTSD CPG mainly strengthens the evidence that was already contained in the 2004 PTSD CPG. According to a VA official, the updated PTSD CPG will include a module on complementary alternative medicine, which was not included in the 2004 PTSD CPG.

[50] In the CPG, cognitive processing therapy is graded a level "A" treatment specifically for female sexual assault-related PTSD. However, VA officials told us that they also consider cognitive processing therapy to be effective for PTSD in veterans. See app. IV for a detailed description of the process used to determine grades for evidence-based recommendations.

[51] Two other psychotherapies, stress inoculation training and eye movement desensitization and reprocessing, were also graded as level "A" treatments for PTSD in the 2004 PTSD CPG, but were not included in the Handbook.

[52] Institute of Medicine, Treatment of Posttraumatic Stress Disorder: An Assessment of the Evidence (Washington, D.C., 2008). The Institute of Medicine is an independent, nonprofit organization that works outside of government to provide authoritative advice to decision makers and the public. The Institute of Medicine found that exposure therapies, including prolonged exposure therapy and elements of cognitive processing therapy, are efficacious treatments for PTSD.

[53] VA officials reported that incorporating cognitive processing therapy and prolonged exposure therapy into the Handbook helped ensure that clinicians who had been trained in these therapies prior to development of the Handbook would be able to offer and provide them in VA facilities as needed. In May 2010, VA's Office of Inspector General reported that as of November 17, 2009, the total number of mental health practitioners who had completed either the cognitive processing therapy or the prolonged exposure therapy training was 3,086. See Department of Veterans Affairs, Office of Inspector General, Healthcare Inspection: Progress in Implementing the Veterans Health Administration's Uniform Mental Health Services Handbook (Washington, D.C., 2010).

[54] To help implement VA's Comprehensive Veterans Health Administration Strategic Plan for Mental Health Services (November 2004), VA allocated additional resources to fund mental health strategic plan initiatives in fiscal years 2005 and 2006. According to VA officials, a part of these additional resources was used to pay for the national cognitive processing therapy and prolonged exposure therapy training programs until the costs of the programs could be integrated into VA's congressional budget submission.

[55] However, VA officials provided documentation regarding consultation with experts and a list of VA entities that participated in reviewing the Handbook.

[56] According to VA officials, VA policies must be recertified every 5 years to remain in effect. The Handbook must be recertified on or before September 2013.

End Note for Appendix III

[1] The study team may also include a health economist, in cases where a CSP proposal involves economic analysis. In addition, the principal investigator may ask the Clinical Science Director to allow other consultants to be a part of the study team, as necessary.

End Note for Appendix IV

[1] Evidence-based care refers to approaches that have consistently been shown in controlled research to be effective for a particular condition or conditions. The VA/DOD Evidence-Based Practice Work Group makes decisions about which clinical practice guidelines for specific conditions will be developed and oversees their development. As of August 2010, the VA/DOD Evidence-Based Practice Work Group had issued 24 CPGs on conditions such as chronic heart failure and major depressive disorder. Since VA and DOD issue the CPGs in a joint effort, they are intended to be used by both VA and DOD clinicians. The VA/DOD Evidence-Based Practice Work Group is supported by VA's Office of Quality and Performance and the U.S. Army Medical Department's Office of Quality Management.

[2] In addition, representatives from VA's Office of Patient Care Services are responsible for identifying VA and DOD clinical leaders.

[3] VA and DOD designees from the VA/DOD Evidence-Based Practice Work Group, with assistance from VA's Office of Patient Care Services, are responsible for selecting the VA and DOD clinical leaders and the evidence chaperone. In addition, they also select another member of the VA/DOD Evidence-Based Practice Work Group to monitor the development of the CPG.

[4] The facilitator is also responsible for keeping the guideline working group focused during meetings and to ensure that it focuses on the quality of research outcomes when formulating evidence-based recommendations in the CPG.

[5] The post-traumatic stress disorder CPG is formally known as The VA/DOD Clinical Practice Guideline for the Management of Post-Traumatic Stress (January 2004).

[6] According to a VA official, an external evidence center is used to minimize bias.

[7] The evidence center provides summaries of research of lower quality only if no higher-quality research is available.

[8] The U.S. Preventive Services Task Force was first convened by the Department of Health and Human Services' Public Health Service in 1984, and since 1998 has been sponsored by the Department of Health and Human Services' Agency for Healthcare Research and Quality. The U.S. Preventive Services Task Force uses explicit criteria to grade the scientific evidence for a broad range of clinical services and develop evidence-based recommendations for clinicians and health systems. While the U.S. Preventive Services Task Force updated its criteria in May 2007, the VA/DOD Evidence-Based Practice Work Group currently uses U.S. Preventive Services Task Force criteria developed prior to May 2007.

[9] The overall quality of the research is considered "good" when the research outcomes are consistent from a number of higher-level research studies and have been conducted across a broad range of populations, thereby providing a high degree of confidence that the research outcomes are true. A "fair" overall quality indicates that the research outcomes could have been a result of true effects or biases present across some or all of the research studies. A "poor" rating for overall quality indicates that any conclusion about the research outcomes is uncertain because of serious methodological shortcomings, sparse data, or inconsistent results.

[10] The net effect of the intervention of research outcomes that are found to be of poor overall quality is not assessed because the evidence is insufficient to make a recommendation for or against routinely providing the intervention.

INDEX

I

J

L

M

N

O

P

Q

R

S

T

U

V

W